Praise for *The Success Gu*

T0022495

"Elizabeth helps us understand that success is a
individuals striving to achieve it. This is a must-read for all to pursue a life
that resonates with your genuine happiness while dismantling the obstacles
that have been holding you back."

> —**Jack Canfield,** coauthor of the #1 *New York Times* bestselling
> Chicken Soup for the Soul series and *The Success Principles:*
> *How to Get from Where You Are to Where You Want to Be*

"Elizabeth Hamilton-Guarino hit a home run with this book; you get a
blueprint for success and different ways to achieve success. Get your notepad ready as you get a master class with this book."

> —**Edwin Thompson,** head baseball coach, Georgetown University

"I truly believe this book is a masterpiece! For anyone who seriously would
like to experience success, sit down and apply yourself to the process Elizabeth has outlined and you will, at the very minimum, know what success
means to you. You may potentially even find that you are more successful
than you ever dreamed possible."

> —**Barbara Wainwright,** author, speaker, and founder of Wainwright
> Global Institute for Professional Coaching

"In this, the latest literary gift from Elizabeth Hamilton-Guarino, you
will readily see the gift is multi-fold. In reading her book, not only will
you receive the wisdom and genuine, generous presence of someone who
deeply wishes you to have the greatest success possible, you will feel yourself uplifted by your own power to achieve it."

> —**Michael McGlone,** actor, writer, and singer

"*The Success Guidebook* ends the practice of constantly shifting the finish
line, which only results in long-term dissatisfaction and longing. Elizabeth
completely redefines the concept of 'success' by showing you how to make
your own definition and set achievable goals that will fulfill your purpose."

> —**Amy Lyle,** comedienne and author, not necessarily in that order

"By diving into this book, you've already gotten your first win! Elizabeth's insights in *The Success Guidebook* will help you to create a plan of action that leads to your desired goals and also gives you the strength to adjust and pivot when needed. The lessons within will remind you to celebrate your successes, big and small."

—**David Meltzer,** legendary sports executive, bestselling author, speaker, and investor

"*The Success Guidebook* is a curation of wisdom from those who have gone out and done it. Packed with gems, Elizabeth has managed to create the full 360 on the elements to create success in your life and career with actionable insights set into stories from people around the globe. A must-read."

—**Indiana Gregg,** founder and CEO of Wedo.ai

"Whenever great people come together, great things happen. That is exactly what has happened here thanks to Elizabeth Hamilton-Guarino. This book is full of some of the most iconic and influential people in their fields, sharing such wisdom, truth, experience, philosophies, and passions. Well worth the time to read and see what either inspires you, or the changes you may need to make for a better and healthier future."

—**Brian J. Esposito,** entrepreneur and founder of Esposito Intellectual Enterprises

"An inspiring page-turner, Elizabeth Hamilton-Guarino's *The Success Guidebook,* is a master class to visualize success—no matter where you are in life. Her transformative Ten Factors of Success are an ideal recipe for self-empowerment to become your Best Ever You!"

—**Kelly Browne,** author of *101 Ways to Create Mindful Forgiveness* and *101 Ways to Say Thank You*

"Dream big, achieve greatness, and live life to the fullest. In *The Success Guidebook,* Elizabeth masterfully lays out the blueprint of what it takes to become successful. For the first time, achieving world-class success is simplified. It's not easy, but it's worth it. This book will change your perspective and inspire you to make a greater impact on the world than you ever imagined."

—**Jesse Cole,** owner of The Savannah Bananas

THE
SUCCESS
GUIDEBOOK

How to Visualize, Actualize, and Amplify You

Elizabeth Hamilton-Guarino

Foreword by Sophia A. Nelson, bestselling author of
The Woman Code and *Be the One You Need*

Health Communications, Inc.
Boca Raton, Florida
www.hcibooks.com

Other Books by Elizabeth Hamilton-Guarino

For Adults

PERCOLATE: Let Your Best Self Filter Through

The Change Guidebook: How to Align Your Heart, Truths, and Energy to
Find Success in All Areas of Your Life

Best Ever You: 52-Week Journal to Your Bravest, Boldest You

For Children

Blueberry and Jam: Adventures in Maine

A Lesson for Every Child: Learning About Food Allergies

Dream Big with Food Allergies

Best Ever You

Dream Big

Self-Confident Sandy

Pinky Doodle Bug

Pinky Doodle Dance

**Library of Congress Cataloging-in-Publication Data
is available through the Library of Congress**

©2024 Elizabeth Hamilton-Guarino

ISBN-13: 978-07573-2480-2 (Paperback)
ISBN-10: 07573-2480-0 (ppb (Paperback)
ISBN-13: 978-07573-2481-9 (ePub)
ISBN-10: 07573-2485-1 (ePub)

HCI, its logos, and marks are trademarks of Health Communications, Inc.

Publisher: Health Communications, Inc.
301 Crawford Boulevard, Suite 200
Boca Raton, FL 33432-3762

Cover, interior design and formatting by Larissa Hise Henoch.

DEDICATION

* * * *

This book is for the
Seekers,
Dreamers,
Thinkers,
Doers,
Believers,
Challengers,
Changers,
and
Those who want to be their best.

Pave your path to success and peace.
Let your dreams fly!

CONTENTS

● ● ●

Best Ever You

I believe most of us are soul-searching.

We are searching for an alignment to purpose for what we truly love to do.

I believe we must visualize our success.

I believe we must actualize what matters most.

I believe we must amplify success with action.

When these things align, the possibilities are endless.

Create awesomeness within.

Become your Best Ever You.

FOREWORD

• • •

Success Is How You Define It

Success. What a powerful and yet at times truly daunting word. When Elizabeth asked me to write the foreword for this amazing book, I had to sit and really think about how I define success in my own life and in the lives of others in my closest personal and professional circles.

What I quickly realized was that success is a profoundly personal word that combines our deepest hopes, dreams, and desires all folded under one big umbrella. But here's the thing: success for me may not be success for you. And that is where I would like to start.

The best piece of advice I can give to you as you approach this new guidebook is that my greatest successes have come from my deepest failures, stumbles, and stops in life. And from those stumbles and stops, I have learned never to measure my own life's journey by the successes or failures of others. To never look at the "greener grass" in someone else's yard, instead of simply focusing on the grass in my own yard that simply needs some love, attention, and weeding. Success is how you define it for yourself. Success is what you make of life. Success should never be defined by others. Success starts within and by knowing your value and worth.

This timely and much-needed book takes the concept of success and uses the stories and journeys of amazing people who have walked it out through some of life's most unthinkable curveballs. People who have been resilient again and again. People who have lost everything, and who, despite it all, still found a way to live out loud in a way that truly inspires us all.

So, what can you say about someone like Elizabeth? She is a whirlwind of positive energy and inspiration. She pours out all she has not just into her successful marriage, or her four handsome and successful sons, but into the rest of us as well. She works tirelessly to lift women, in particular, with her Best Ever You Network, and she is always collaborating on projects to lift us higher as human beings. That is why I wholeheartedly endorse this book and cannot wait for you to read it. To ingest it. To sit with it. And most importantly, to walk it out in your day-to-day living, laughing, loving, and learning. This is by far, in my humble opinion, one of her best collaborative works yet.

Let me end where I began—this book will change your life. But only if you are willing to put in the work and work the great nuggets of wisdom shared throughout this timely and inspirational book. So, what is success again, Sophia? I'm glad you asked. Success is living the life you want authentically, boldly, and with power. With grace. With confidence. And with purpose.

You can do this. All you need is a dream, some discipline, and a little bit of bravery, too!

—Sophia A. Nelson, Esq.
Bestselling author of *The Woman Code* and *Be the One You Need*

ACKNOWLEDGMENTS

● ● ●

I believe books have wings. They arrive in your hands, on your doorstep, or into your heart and soul just when needed. I'd like to begin by thanking everyone who has not only found my books, but also shared them with others. I write for those who need or crave information about self-love, self-worth, navigating purpose, gratitude, energy, time-management, change, success, and being your best.

In my own exciting moment of my books getting their wings, while on a trip to Massachusetts, I randomly sat next to a group of twenty-something women. I couldn't help but overhear their conversation about their moms, who were leaving self-help books around for them to read and them not liking any of them. Then one said, "I did like this one about change, called *The Change Guidebook*." I nearly passed out hearing that. (That is the book I wrote before the one you are reading now.)

A darling brunette picked up her phone and showed the others next to her the book on Amazon. Then very quietly behind my sunglasses, my ripped jeans, and with my hair not done, I said to myself, *I'm the author of the book they are all chatting about so kindly and I can't believe this is happening right now!* I love how the Universe graces us in the most unexpected ways. Then I quietly told one of the girls that I am the author. This was followed by some screams that I'm not used to as a mom of four sons, and photos. It was a serendipitous and meaningful moment to have as a fan and developer of people.

To you the readers and sharers, thank you. I love this process of people finding my books and information and being an author and the founder of The Best Ever You Network. I'm grateful to the network for all of the love and support you give me!

Then there are those who include you when you least expect it. An author friend of mine sent me a link and said, "Congratulations!!!!" I replied, "For what?" and she said, "Look, *The Change Guidebook* is on this incredible list." The book was included by *Good Housekeeping* magazine as one of the "18 Best Self-Love Books" for 2023. This was a dream come true. To see my book alongside some of the greatest books on that topic was a moment I will never forget. So thank you to Marisa LaScala and Lizz Schumer and *Good Housekeeping* magazine for including me on this prestigious list.

The support crew of my husband and four sons continues to listen to my varying degrees of great and not-so-great ideas. They are a constant source of love and encouragement, who always amaze me with their own joy, success, and compassion for each other and the world. Since my last book, we have two new dogs, Harley and Bahama. They are an endless supply of joy and warm writer's feet. The three cats continue to trade off sitting on my computer or notebooks, making it impossible to write on some days. I've learned to read the room, take their hints, and just take a break often in the sun. My dad would have loved to continue to see me put books out into the world that help people the way they do. I believe he's always with me. My mom is proud and guides our family. Thank you always.

I couldn't have a better team to help me be successful than the team at HCI. Christine Belleris, Christian Blonshine, Lindsey Triebel, Larissa Henoch, Mary Ellen Hettinger, and my agent Steve Harris. Thank you. You all make every moment better and I'm so proud to be working with the same team once again to bring you this book. Your expertise and kindness show why you are a guide to many in this industry and I thank my lucky stars for you every day.

Thank you to the friends who viewed and edited this in real time and provided valuable feedback and edits. A very special thank-you to Jennifer Vaughn for you being you and for being such a wonderful friend and who often has "words." You are one of the most gifted writers on the planet. Barbara Wainwright, your oversight on the exercises in this book was so helpful; thank you for being such a wonderful friend and mentor all of these years. Amy Lyle, you are one funny lady. Thank you for the humor and jokes along the way. Laughter is such an important component of life.

I wouldn't be where I am today without the help of Pat and Ruth McLeaney. They took me in when I needed it most and helped me become a college graduate and find success in my twenties.

My gratitude to the following for sharing their stories with us and helping bring this book to life: Jack Canfield, Sophia A. Nelson, Jesse and Emily Cole, The Savannah Bananas, Miriam Laundry, Nando Cesarone, Rhys Olivia Cote, Coach Edwin Thompson, Cam Guarino, Michael McGlone, Jennifer Vaughn, Linda Pritchett, Julie Beth Bruckman, Indiana Gregg, Del Duduit, former Congressman Ric Keller, Brian J. Esposito, E. J. Yerzak, Lisa Gable, Tina Sloan, Liz Brunner, Mitch Gaylord, Kelly Browne, Juli Ann Polise, Helen Polise, Amy Lyle, Gary Kobat, Quaid Guarino, Dr. Serena H. Huang, Dr. Ivan Misner, Emily A. Francis, Merril Hoge, Sally Huss, Kate Glendon, Wayne and Sherri Connell, Mark and Gail Elvidge, and Vermont Nut Free Chocolates.

I'm so honored to know you all and see all you do in the world to help people be their best.

Love, Elizabeth

INTRODUCTION

● ● ●

Why *The Success Guidebook?*

Did you know you already ARE wildly and amazingly successful? Do you see it? Most people don't, and that's why we are here. It's time to stop spinning your wheels and over-working for a fragile concept that feels unattainable. It's time to redefine success for yourself so it becomes meaningful to you. This book will help you go inward, upward, and outward to see it, be it, and do it—to fully understand how you can live a life most authentically and aligned with you.

The heartfelt experiences, concepts, steps, strategies, factors, and insights in this book are here to help, inspire, teach, and reveal to you how to live your life to the fullest. For many years I have been observing the top factors of success and how they manifest in each of us; why we struggle to identify them, and how we keep them. As the founder of The Best Ever You Network, master coach, and author of multiple bestselling and award-winning books on the topic of change and success management, I remain dedicated to helping others become their best.

In this book you will learn to maintain and sustain your vision for what success looks like for you personally, professionally, and confidently redefined. You'll feel proud and valuable, rather than searching and seeking thing after thing after thing and always feeling less than. Within the pages of this book, you will learn to feel successful without the overwhelming drive for whatever society defines as "success" that so often overrides so many aspects of our personal lives. This book will focus on personal and professional success—together—not one sacrificed for the other.

We'll look at success as multidimensional and very closely associated with ten factors which, when followed, consistently have life-changing and lasting results. This book will reveal the characteristics and actions linked to performance and personal results at a variety of levels and help you hone your ability to tap into them, even when life gets tricky.

Success isn't one-size-fits-all. I believe traditional measurements for success are unrealistic and often feel largely unattainable. These mental, emotional, physical, and spiritual disconnects have created multiple issues on many fronts. We need a new way forward: a new definition of success that is individualized. Here you have your best awareness, an important characteristic for excelling in all areas of your life at a world-class level.

Remember, breakthroughs happen when truth intersects with infinite possibilities. Gaining access to success can be like unlocking a galaxy you've never seen before, that grants you heightened thoughts and attention on various areas of your life. Perhaps it's health, relationships, confidence, or the freedom of personal space you've sacrificed in previous pursuits of success that have become dull or fractured. Imagine pursuing the life of your dreams by also giving attention comprehensively to all areas of your life, such as health or relationships, which can suffer when attention is paid in such a focused manner to another area in the pursuit of an old definition of "success." This book will hold your hand and guide you as you discover the results you seek are well within the scope of your capabilities—and, actually, already within you.

Success has an energy to it, and when you're in the presence of someone who demonstrates it, the construct is palpable. The person isn't necessarily famous, wealthy, or known to the world, but the aura is magnetic. They are focused and tenacious, yet calm. They exude confidence and self-assured-ness. Mind you, it is a well-honed skill, and one you will learn to replicate here and translate to multiple areas of your life.

It can be scary to think you really can have it all, but I assure you, if you started today—right now, actually—and lifted the shroud of confusion, fear, frustration, and discontent in yourself and instead operated within the various areas of your life by visualizing, actualizing, and amplifying the success you seek, just imagine the life you could have!

As you navigate chapter by chapter, the framework of world-class excellence will build, as others share how they've amplified it in their own excellence. You'll learn to take the power away from pain and setbacks so they can no longer define your future. We will work together to have strength to finally remove those stubborn stumbling blocks holding you back from a life filled with bold new possibilities. You will find your excellence, clarity, purpose, and confidence to once and for all become everything you were born to be. This book will guide you through new principles of thoughts, words, and deeds that enlighten and elevate. The sooner you start, the quicker the breakthrough to your best success.

In my coaching practice, I see a pattern of people whose confidence has been chipped at or ripped away or those who think their situation or past will prevent their success. Remember a time in your life where you've been rejected for one reason or another? Our lives aren't complete without obstacles. These situations and people create hurdles of doubt and other problems that we have to learn to leap over with grace—sometimes as fast as we can.

I sure have had plenty of these moments and am shouting from the rooftops for all to hear that now is the moment to stop giving these folks and situations any more room in your heart, mind, and soul. *The Success Guidebook* will help you stop feeling like you have to prove your worth to others or prove people wrong. You'll align with and understand your real self once and for all.

Often, encounters such as rejection or rivalry, or even society in general, can fuel you. They make you feel like you need to prove something to someone or perhaps yourself, only to really understand that success is so much more than proving people wrong. It's also more than conventional measurements such as data or the dollars in your bank account. Especially as we age or have a setback, we come to terms that success is something far greater and something that just can't simply be measured. For me, true success is reflected in the smiles that brighten our faces and the peace that settles in our hearts. Success grows from rooting our lives in gratitude, focusing our intention, and putting forth actions into being our very best. In seeking gratitude through intention and action, success is revealed in each moment.

All of these best practices and concepts matter more than any dollar or traditional measurement mostly because we aren't entitled to time. This concept hit me like a freight train when my father had a series of strokes and ultimately passed away. After seeing him so ill and then seeing him take his last breath, for quite a while after that moment, my perspective on life shifted dramatically. It was like my entire way of life was jarred into this realization that the most unsuccessful day you will ever have in your life is the day you stop breathing. It sucks that it has to be that way, but wow, it is more important than ever to pause, understand your value and "enough-ness," and really be judicious in how you spend your moments. Also, within those moments, when you root in gratitude and benchmark your success with it, you will arrive in each moment authentically and aligned with your purpose for being here.

It's time to finally overcome anything holding you back and harness the power of YOU to move forward with alignment, clarity, purpose, and incredible confidence to be bold, brave, and open to this concept of unlimited possibilities. Together, we'll reveal the whys and motivations unique to each of you and how to override aspects of your life that may be hindering your success. Explore, understand, relate, and revise, now—once and for all—because success waits for no one. You were born with specific superpowers; let them reveal themselves and shine bright.

Remember: shine bright. Live your superpowers.

My Story

I've had moments in my life when my superpower wasn't earning money. In fact, my pockets were lined with lint balls, and I didn't quite know where my next dollar was coming from. A few of these moments have had a lasting and profound impact on me.

I learned the value of money, in terms of success, at a young age. I grew up in Pleasant Valley, Iowa, in a huge family of ten kids raised by entrepreneurial parents who had a string of successful businesses. In 1984, when I was around age fourteen, we hit the big time with a chain of video stores we owned. My parents expanded the business and we lived very comfortably. I was in high school and on to college at The University of Iowa, and things were great for several years—until they weren't. The Movie Stores of Iowa and Illinois gradually were no longer a thing. My parents were defrauded by someone they trusted and that resulted in a series of events that ultimately placed the company into a sudden bankruptcy restructuring, which then progressed to a bankruptcy liquidation.

It was devastating to everyone and personally left me totally lost at that time, as my only job experience was in the video rental business and at such a young age, I no longer had financial security and my parents to count on. I was in denial and disbelief. It was heartbreaking to see our family's work come to a crushing close.

I haven't told very many people this: at the age of eighteen, mostly from sheer sadness and possibly madness from these events, I slept in a car for several days, not admitting and basically pretending that nothing was wrong. I certainly had plenty of places where I could have gone. I had plenty of friends and people I could have probably relied on but felt like I needed to figure this out on my own. My parents had left Iowa during the bankruptcy proceedings and moved to Minnesota. I chose to stay in Iowa. Our house in Iowa was available to live in for a small period of time, however, it became obvious that I needed to think and act fast to find a place to live and a way to support myself.

Everything I had known, including the house that I had lived in since second grade, was all gone. Homes on Lake Vermillion in Minnesota, boats, and everything we knew and had were basically gone in what felt like a flash. I distanced myself from the events in order to put one foot in front of the other and move forward.

We were no longer that rich, huge family. No more country clubs and everything paid for, including college. I was on my own. When I saw the award-winning TV series *Schitt's Creek,* honestly, I could relate so much in many ways. Similar to the first episode of *Schitt's Creek,* I had gathered up all my rich stuff to be poor and on my own struggling. I quickly moved into a storage facility converted into studio units in a safe-enough space, but very unlike the posh mansion I was moving from. There definitely was no doorman looking at who was coming and going. It could have been worse. It was the best I could do with what I knew at the time.

It was in these moments that I did not quit. Instead, I asked myself, *What am I going to do with my life?* I began a quest to learn how to survive, thrive, stand on my own two feet, and become successful.

I have worked hard ever since to become the best version of myself that I possibly could be, as it became clear that I was going to have to earn everything, and it wasn't going to be easy. The days of my parents paying for everything I could dream of were over. It became very important to me to learn how to roll with a punch, overcome struggles, and learn to have compassion for myself and for all around me, since it became clear that many had troubles that appeared to be far greater than mine.

Fast-forward many years. When our youngest son, Quaid, went to first grade, I decided it was time to dig my business suits out of the closet and go back to work. I became the vice president of a financial services firm. I quickly discovered it was impossible, for me personally, to be great at being both a mom and being employed outside the house. It felt like I was sharply divided in two or even three with being a mom, wife, and now working outside the house. There was also no time for myself, and having friends sounded even more exhausting. That's what I became: exhausted, followed by extremely frustrated, and then a bit jealous of how everyone but me seemed to be able to "do it all."

I wondered how in the world my mom and dad had achieved so much with ten kids and how they kept it all together even with all that happened! This experience gave me a deeper appreciation for everyone juggling their various aspects of life and helped me begin to define success in that moment for *myself*. I felt like an utter failure in many ways. For us, with four young boys and their needs coming first, we were easily derailed when someone would become ill or need something that clashed with work. That doesn't even include if me or my husband would get sick or if I would get one of my migraines that I was prone to. I just couldn't do it all. It's when I stopped counting our blessings and lost sight of all the positives that my husband and I caught ourselves and course corrected.

What I learned in these moments is that I really wanted to be at home and find a way to work from home. That way at least one of us was available and present for whatever the kids needed. While contemplating my options, one day I closed my office door and began to brainstorm. I figured if this struggle to juggle it all was happening to us, it was happening to others. In an effort to figure out how to be my best moving forward, I wrote down the words, *Best Ever You*. And in that moment, The Best Ever You Network was born. I quit my job on the spot. I went home and asked a neighbor to help me register the domain and put up a small website and the next day it was up and running. I've glossed over the part where everyone except my husband, kids, and neighbor thought I was totally nuts, especially when I said I wanted to become an author of self-help books and host a radio show. I had a vision, and I ran with it, even if nobody could see it in those moments but me.

Since then, Best Ever You has grown into a recognized brand that continues to shine: a website, a large social media following, bestselling books, *Best Ever You Magazine*, master classes, life coach certification courses, and *The Best Ever You Show*, my podcast, which has hundreds of guests and millions of downloads. I'm endlessly grateful for the growth I've experienced.

My intentions and purpose remain genuine and clear: to help as many people as possible live their best and most positive, peaceful, successful lives. It's nonstop learning and a success curve that has had its ups and downs.

Fast-forward again to today. I'm in my mid-fifties at the time of this book. I feel successful. Here's why: first, I think even if I have a positive impact on only one person, I'm successful. Second, I personally redefined success for myself long ago, and I always vowed to measure it differently. Neither money nor fame can make you happy. I look back on the money we had growing up but realize that tending to the business took up a lot of my parents' time, and I wish I'd seen them more. Getting my health under control and seeming to age out of migraines associated with hormone fluctuations has been one of the absolute best feelings of success ever. Freedom from that acute pain and exhaustion, and the consistency that comes with feeling well, has been the key to me feeling vibrant, confident, happy . . . and so much more.

When I think about my life and success, what comes instantly to mind is my husband of over twenty-five years, Peter, and our four sons, family, friends, and our lives together. Success to me is in the relationships you have, the bonds you create, the network, and collaborations, and treating everyone you encounter with a sense of grace, compassion, elegance, kindness, peace, and genuine interest. You most certainly don't know what people are going through as you encounter them, unless you stop to pause and ask in great detail while listening with an open heart and mind.

Success will never solely be the dollars in your bank account or the toys you have. I love this quote from the late, great UCLA basketball coach John Wooden, who said, "I knew what success was not. I didn't see recommendations, promotions, points, scores, trophies, medals, and money as accurate measurements. Such items may result in status, but status isn't necessarily success." He went on to say, "Success is peace of mind that is the direct result of self-satisfaction in knowing you did your best to become the best that you are capable of being." In his book, *Pyramid of Success,* Wooden advises us not to focus on being better than someone else, but rather to strive to be the best you can be. I agree with Coach Wooden, who never had a win-at-all-costs approach. It's up to each of us to understand and celebrate our unique talents and gifts and how to bring them to the world.

How to Use This Book

This book is divided into three focus areas with ten chapters, each representing a factor of success, followed by exercises to practice the lessons, and journal prompts to elaborate on your thoughts and solidify the ideas. Think of these as true practice areas to put in motion what you learn along the way.

I've also woven in stories from members of The Best Ever You Network who took real action and achieved real success. Each success story highlights how a challenge was overcome and how excellence and success were achieved. You'll see how ordinary shifts to extraordinary, and how the first small sparks of success fires up inspiration to keep going, collaborating, and connecting.

I suggest that you keep a journal or notebook dedicated to your journey. If you don't like to write in your book, all exercises are also conveniently available for download. At the completion of the book, there's an option to submit your work to receive a Best Ever You Success Master Class Certification. Learn more at BestEverYou.com/SuccessGuidebook.

The Ten Factors of Success

My wish for you is to feel success in every moment of your life, no matter the balance in your bank account or the trouble you may be facing. The best measure of success is your smile and others smiling around you.

What follows are the Ten Factors of Success I developed during my many years of working with clients as a master coach and founder of The Best Ever You Network. They are the proven tactics of creative action to help you visualize, actualize, and amplify excellence and success—and make them last. Whether you are dreaming big to achieve the awesomeness within or making a pivot, this process can be used time and time again to achieve the results you seek.

My goal is to help you master the Ten Factors of Success, so that you have the tools to actualize your dreams and goals to amplify professional and personal success. These factors can help you navigate, overcome stubborn obstacles, and harness the power to courageously move forward with clarity, a renewed purpose, and the confidence to build a life of bold and infinite possibilities.

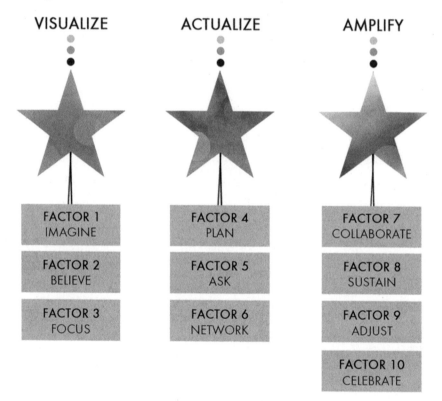

Commit to live differently. Commit to be your best. This is the first step forward, when you listen to that inkling that your best life is just ahead. This book is a key resource in your Best Ever You Toolbox to build your best life and be your best you.

Let's celebrate YOU within these pages.

I sincerely hope you love *The Success Guidebook*. It is from my heart to yours and I wish you the very best success always.

Love, Elizabeth

PART 1

VISUALIZE YOUR SUCCESS

CHAPTER 1
IMAGINE

The First Factor of Success is to imagine. We often have an inkling to do something—which may have started at a very young age—and it is something that only we can see. Pay attention to all of this and don't ignore it. We may need to pivot or change course, but now is the time to follow our passion, dreams, and goals by first seeing it for ourselves. If we can see it, we can be it and do it.

Jesse Cole and his wife Emily had just five months left to go before opening day and they were out of money. They had sold their house and belongings, emptied their bank accounts, and kissed their good credit scores goodbye. The couple had enormous dreams of revolutionizing the game of baseball with a fun, family focus. Their dream was so vivid that they exchanged an easier life for an air mattress on the floor of their dilapidated duplex complete with cockroaches, ramen noodles for dinner with the occasional cracker to ward off hunger pains. Their struggles paid off with what is now a renowned, entertainment-heavy, baseball experience known as The Savannah Bananas. Donning his famous yellow tux, Jesse

Cole is the ringmaster of what is now referred to as a baseball circus that has forever changed the way the sport is played, watched, and loved. Banana Ball plays to sold-out crowds and packed stadiums, is heavy into social media with millions of fans, while breaking the traditional rules of baseball. Banana Ball features dancing players and "The Dancing Ump," trick plays, a two-hour time limit on games, no bunting, batters having the option of trying to steal first, no stepping out of the box, no mound visits, and a scoring system that awards a point to the team that puts up the most runs each inning. My personal favorite is rule number eight: If a fan catches the ball, it's an automatic out. Aside from the wacky rules that turn the traditional game of baseball on its head, there are dances on the field and in the stands and two other opposing teams: the Party Animals and the Firefighters. I was able to see this all for myself when they stopped in Portland, Maine, in 2023. My son Cam and I had full media access to the team. It was quite a treat to see the talent, dedication, vision, personalities, and that "Fans First" motto The Savannah Bananas are now famous for. These days, Jesse and Emily travel the globe with Banana Ball and laugh about the early days when all of it was little more than a dream and a risk. They are proof of how it can happen for you.

SUCCESS TIP #1: See It

If you can't visualize your success, I assure you nobody else can either, so this first step is imperative. Even if you've been dreaming of something your entire life, plans can change and mature. Maybe right now you're considering a pivot to a new endeavor. Maybe you're visualizing your success after an obstacle or setback, such as a health issue. Please understand that whatever your age, location, or other circumstance, imagination can reveal a dream even bigger and bolder than before. Your success starts with visualizing how you'll make that happen.

Success isn't achieved by accident; it starts from within. There are things you can do and best practices to help secure a better position to succeed, but dreams plant the seed. They cost nothing and come without obstacles and hurdles. I remember dreaming of becoming an author. I know others who've had dreams of being a firefighter, model, famous singer, doctor, president, athlete, and whatever else their imaginations could cook up. Dreaming of change won't bring change. Only action will. If you want to change your job, living situation, relationship, or anything that isn't working to be the best it can be, formulate a process, visualize the outcome, and connect to all possibilities.

SUCCESS TIP #2: Be It

Fall in love with what you see unfolding for yourself, as long as it aligns with your authentic vision. It most definitely will cause disruption and change.

For a bunch of years now, I visualized being someplace other than Maine for winter. I created a vision board with shells, beaches, sun, sand, vacation, and a bit of baseball in the mix. (Our son Cam was a graduate student transfer and a lefty pitcher for the Georgetown University Hoyas.)

Gradually the dream came true as we began to take trips here and there during the winter for our son's baseball games. The stays seemed to extend from one week to two.

So when my husband and I announced plans to escape the often brutal Maine winters to snowbird in South Carolina for six or even eight weeks, people thought we couldn't do it and said it was a crazy idea. We got all sorts of feedback that we chose to ignore! However, our sons thought it was a great idea and jumped at the chance to help us. They knew we needed the change and that we'd worked very hard to help them become independent adults. On separate occasions each of our four sons congratulated us on our bold plans and pronounced them "very cool." With their support, we had the confidence to test run our dream for six weeks, counting on each of them to help support the homestead and care for our family pets while we were away. It makes all the difference in the world when you have support—it's the glue that holds success together.

In fact, some of this book was written during our experimental hiatus in South Carolina. Rather than shoveling snow and laying ice melt on our front walkway, we spent February and most of March traveling to watch our son's team compete in Division 1 matchups at the USA Baseball National Training Complex in Cary, North Carolina, and other locations.

SUCCESS TIP #3: Do It

Once you have a vision in your heart and mind, do it! Stick to your vision regardless of the feedback. In my case, because of the energy that was being released from being so clear about the vision we had, I don't think much was stopping our trip to South Carolina. We were doing it. However, sometimes, it's just not that easy to do grand things, including trips. As life continues to teach us along the way, doing grand things means overcoming challenges, especially when there are health issues at play. All the more reason to lean in with that clear vision, anchored in faith, and intuitively just go for it. Don't worry about the how. Just stay focused on the doing and the being.

A few years ago, now, my dear friend, mentor, and world-known Integrative Performance Coach Gary Kobat was recovering from open heart surgery—à la Mick Jagger. A fit, healthy, four-time Team USA athlete in cycling, Gary had no idea he had any heart issues at all, until actor Will Ferrell saved his life by calling 9-1-1 during a training bike ride together in Malibu, California. Will had called Gary to learn how to master, i.e., learn how *not* to be the slowest bike rider of a group of seasoned athlete friends on a three-day bike ride along the Northern California Monterey Coastline. (That's right, an accomplished person calling an accomplished coach for another level of accomplishment, learning, or success in another area.) However, on that day, success meant something else entirely and Gary's life was saved.

While recuperating from a surgery where a person may be on life support for six hours of the operation, and where optimal recovery may still mean strict physical limitations, Gary began to define "success" for himself. It began with the most basic, smallest, and authentic moments—each powerful, valuable, and important to his life. From learning how to sneeze without tearing surgery stitches to putting his socks on by himself, or walking unaided to the bathroom, to Gary each little victory was a grand success to be celebrated. Gary's recuperation and recovery was anchored in his belief, courage, intuition, faith, vision, and desire to live again to the fullest.

Ah yes, and there is his triumphant ATM walk. You see, upon getting home from the hospital, Gary noticed that he only had a few dollars in his "cycling" wallet. (All cyclists carry a few dollars in their wallets, with an ID and insurance card in case of an emergency.) Well, Gary being Gary, and not knowing if he was ever going to walk, ride, run, lift, swim, or race again, decided that he was going to walk to the ATM machine down the street. Yes, that's right, in "just do it" fashion, he told his sister his plan. When she offered him a ride, he responded, "You drive near me, in case this all goes south, *ha-ha*, but I am walking—for the first time, I have to do it."

So he walked. Slowly. Methodically. He arrived at the ATM sweating, somewhat questioning his choices, yet overall confident in them, and he withdrew his $100. Success! His Super Bowl! A hundred dollars! Woohoo! Well, for that day anyway, and for that moment in his life. This grown man, who transforms athletes into gold medal winners, is celebrating a one-block walk as if it's his Olympics. You see, success can be personal, deep, authentic, real, simple, powerful, basic, and may not quite be anything like what you think it is now.

Some people may think you're bananas with your crazy ideas and lofty goals. Here's my advice: Do it anyway! It can get loud and bumpy out there, because success comes with comments and criticism—whether you've asked for them or not. Suddenly, everyone has an opinion about your dream and why it will or won't work. Jesse and Emily Cole were walloped by feedback and still pushed on. Their plans were well underway, and they were announcing the winner of a contest to name the team—The Savannah Bananas—when the naysayers felt obligated to tell them why they would fail, with this sampling of mean-spirited and decidedly unhelpful opinions: "You've lost your minds," and "No one will come," and "This is an awful idea!" When others don't share your vision, it can be frustrating to stick with what only you can conceptualize. But Emily and Jesse persisted, nevertheless. Their gamble and sacrifice paid off and today the Bananas play to full stadiums. This hijinks-filled disruption to traditional baseball is finding a permanent place in sports entertainment that is evolving and growing to include a brand-new generation of fans.

SUCCESS TIP #4: Reach for the Stars

When you reach out to someone you admire as a fan, sometimes you get the coolest responses. As I was just learning about The Savannah Bananas, I became obsessed with so many aspects of the group that I became determined to include Jesse Cole and The Savannah Bananas in this book. This led me down a path of studying the team's baseball shenanigans, how they operate with fans, Jesse's books and philosophy of success, and the way all of it came to be. Due to tour and time constraints as well as their incredible popularity, it's very difficult to land an off-field interview. Jesse and the team were also busy with a world tour. Trying to avoid a "no" response, I visualized courage along with "say yes" vibes and sent him a request for a chat with me—both for this book, and for The Best Ever You Network.

I received that *yes* I was hoping for and in true Bananas' style and honoring the team's motto, Jesse placed me—*the fan*—above all else, and made sure to put on a heck of a show. We had an initial phone call and then taped interviews and arranged for content for this book. We were all in. I promoted his books on Best Ever You, and all of this eventually led to us meeting in person here in Portland, Maine.

When someone you admire treats you that way, you never forget it. Reach for the stars! If *you've* been reached for, reach back and treat people as if they are the superstar. There is no true formula for how the success of these interactions is measured. When Jesse and I treat each other like superstars, the impact of that reaches far behind us, like universal good will more valuable than money.

SUCCESS TIP #5: Redefine Success for Yourself

In my time with Jesse Cole, the concepts that I think about success were reinforced—expanding the definition, standards, and measurements to include things such as happiness, smiles, fun, and laughter.

As I've said, my purpose within these pages is to help us all redefine and measure success in a way that becomes personal rather than a one-size-fits-all concept.

To define success for yourself, it is important to understand what motivates and inspires you, while accepting that your definition may change over time. For example, had you asked me what success is when I was twenty-one, I probably would have said things like having money, career, a house, and such. Ask me when I was thirty-two, and I might have told you simply getting dressed for the day, as I had four children ages newborn to eight at that time. And now, with my boys grown and flown, my interests have continued to evolve.

Here's my own definition:

Success is reflected in the smiles that brighten your face and the peace that settles in your heart. It's finding gratitude in all things as well as intention and actions to be your very best in each moment.

When I work with my clients, here are some questions I ask them:
- Have you ever thought about what success really means to you?
- What do you dream of doing?
- It's true the possibilities are endless, but what lengths are you going to go to, to achieve success?
- What is your why?
- If I say the words, "Yay, you!" what am I celebrating with you?
- Do you realize you are already enough? What does that mean to you?

I could ask these questions to one thousand people and get one thousand different answers. Here's the thing with success: it's all over the place and it is personal to you. In my heart, I believe success is a misunderstood, mismeasured, and misaligned word. Many of us even misconstrue success to fit a narrative we are forcing ourselves to believe. Modern measurements of success need to change to fit the needs of today's world. We are pushing the boundaries of what is practical, obtainable, and that which creates and fosters well-being for ourselves and society.

SUCCESS TIP #6: Trade Gripes for Gratitude

When you trade gripes for gratitude and create an operational foundation of gratitude in your life, your entire being will shift into abundance. It's hard to not feel successful when you feel abundant. It's when you feel negative, stuck, and perhaps lacking that the feelings of "not enough" come forward and try to take over as CEO of your life. Trust me, it's not how you want to operate. I'm suggesting you make some trades. It's time to take a look at your behavior, attitude, actions, beliefs, values, and goals, and make a shift! This is a moment for you to gather up the bad actors in your life (fear, failure, stuckness, blame, toxic thoughts, gripes, groans, whining, complaining, overdoing it, and whatever else that drags your beautiful, authentic, enough-self down), and full on insert some incredible positive energy. Let learning, action, accountability, responsibility, trust, gratitude, sleep, rest, clarity, joy, and love take center stage, for they are acclaimed actors. It may take practice! Catch yourself and trade up those gripes for positive actions and self-talk for your best success. Can you think of any line of thinking that you have that you'd like to change?

SUCCESS TIP #7: Work for It

My *4-4-4 Newsletter* is intended to help people change to operate their lives with more thought to themselves and the world. Each week I provide subscribers with four ideas for themselves, four ideas for humanity, four journal prompts, and four affirmations. It sparks creativity and change.

Most of the people that seek my help are looking to navigate change and success. It's usually one of those two things, or both, because they are intimately linked and affect all areas of your life. As I wrote in *The Change Guidebook*, I believe one's ability to learn about and navigate change is a must for your Best Ever You Toolbox. One of the things that I see repeatedly is people putting all their energy into one area of their life which then causes multiple other areas of their life to suffer. It creates a wacky imbalance in life that is hard to navigate and manage, one with regrets and cases of the shoulda, coulda, wouldas.

Take my client, Trisha, who arrived at my coaching with a marriage on the brink of divorce. She had a wonderful career and lots to show for it, but her travel schedule meant she was seldom home. Another client, Samantha, a millionaire who was diagnosed with cancer and felt so stressed and unhealthy that her life, she told me, felt like it was unraveling. Both women's lives were out of balance in terms of comprehensive success. We worked together and started right away on that aspect of healing and bringing things back in check, before we could even begin to think about wrapping success back in. As I kept seeing this over and over, I developed a way to help people incorporate well-rounded success into their lives.

Comprehensive or well-rounded success is attainable and more realistic than focusing on just one area. It's time to pay attention to all areas of your life so, for example, you don't wake up one day with all the money you dreamed of earning, yet you missed most of the major milestones in your kids' lives, or you've worked so hard that you're too unhealthy to enjoy the spoils of achievement. We want to prevent the sting of regret and "If only I would have . . ." where possible.

One thing is certain: dreaming and imagining come first. In order to actualize your success, you must first *see* it happening for yourself. Let's start there, with how to make it so clear you can see the future from a mile away.

I believe we as a society must make a shift to endless possibilities for success with values, beliefs, and actions that aren't detrimental or destructive to every aspect of our well-being. It's time for new definitions of what success is, what it isn't, and to have a full understanding ahead of time of the sacrifices and damaging results you can achieve when you put one-track, superstar-or-bust blinders on.

Success is unpredictable in ways that common themes or threads cannot embrace, therefore, the work we'll do here will help update success to mean something different for everyone. Success is dependent upon our individual capabilities, struggles, and personal attachment to end results that yield emotions and feelings solely unique to each person.

While it would be simple to visualize success, snap a finger, and watch it take shape before your eyes, it's going to take work. The factors that build success, including thinking about what it means to you, require learning and changing perceptions you have likely held for your entire life. Having status, money, awards, or famous contacts in your phone is not the key to success. To find success, let's talk about happiness in *all* areas of your life.

The concept of absorbing achievement may mean reflecting upon it to ensure you're stepping in the right direction. Give yourself a chance to examine the place you're moving into. It is important to know when you are stepping in the right direction.

In this next section, you'll meet Nando Cesarone and Rhys Olivia Cote, who are generously sharing how visualizing and imagining their success has worked for them.

First, let's meet Nando Cesarone, UPS Executive Vice President and President of US Operations. I'm very honored to share his story here with you and know you'll find him as inspiring as I do.

The son of Italian immigrants, Nando Cesarone learned early on the value of hard work and determination. His father, envisioning a better life for his family, moved from Italy to Canada as a tailor and eventually ran a shoe business—a job that meant long hours. Once Nando was old enough, he began working in the family business after school. He considers his father the biggest influence on his life. He started at UPS as a part-time employee seeking tuition reimbursement and spending money. A manager saw something in him and helped him realize his potential. As one role grew into another, Nando imagined a bigger and better future for himself and his family. On the professional front, roles over his long career included building teams from the ground up, around the world. There was adversity along the way, but success meant maintaining a clear vision to overcome those challenges. These experiences also made him realize that as a leader, he needed to pay it forward and provide an environment where his team could self-actualize and visualize their own success. More than three decades, a dozen assignments, and four international moves later, he heads US and airline operations for the world's largest transportation company, helping UPS move our world forward by delivering what matters.

Stories from the Heart

Nando Cesarone—Imagining a Better Future

I learned about the power of imagination from my dad. It was post-World War II Italy, and Europe was still rebuilding. Jobs were hard to come by, and he wanted a better life for himself and my mom. He decided they needed to leave Italy and plant roots somewhere new. He imagined a place where they could start a new life and ensure more opportunity for our family—and he brought that vision to life.

My parents chose Toronto, Ontario, Canada, as their new home. A tailor by trade, my dad found a job and began saving to bring my mom over. It took three years of hard work and careful saving, but he did it. My mom made the trek to Toronto.

Fast-forward a few years and three sons later, my father's dedication hadn't waned. The life he imagined for us required working multiple jobs, and he was willing to do whatever it took to provide for us, but it meant I didn't see him much.

He eventually started a shoe business, and when I was old enough, I'd work with him on the weekends. I enjoyed it because I got to see how he worked and how he figured things out. And most of all, it allowed us to spend time together and just talk. I didn't know it then, but those times would become some of my dearest memories of my dad.

During our talks in the shoe shop, he would give me advice and had some favorite words of wisdom and sayings. Some are not appropriate for print here—he was a passionate Italian, after all! But two things stick out in my mind: "Easy jobs don't pay much," and "Whatever you do, outwork those around you, and do it right."

My dad lived by those words, especially because he wanted to pay for a college education for each of his three boys. It worked out for my brothers, but then the shoe business closed. When it was my turn, my parents were unable to pay for me.

I remember when my dad delivered the news. He did it with so much compassion and grace. I know now that it was harder on him than it was on me, and looking back, I think it broke his heart.

That conversation brought us closer, and maybe more importantly, taught me two lessons that I still live by today.

1. **True leadership requires empathy.** The way my dad spoke that day inspired my leadership style, with empathy as its cornerstone. That talk has become the blueprint for me whenever I'm headed into a tough conversation, and it's my formula for setting an example for others to see the importance of empathy. My dad thought that conversation would weaken our relationship. Instead, it taught me how empathy can strengthen bonds of trust.

2. **If you're achieving everything you ever dreamed of, think bigger.** When reality doesn't meet your imagination, it doesn't mean you've failed. In my dad's case, he imagined big, bold, amazing things. He strove beyond his station, punched above his weight, and accomplished incredible feats—even if it wasn't every single thing he imagined. At UPS, we call this "constructive dissatisfaction." There is always something bigger and bolder to imagine, and it drives us to be better than we ever thought possible.

Visualizing Next Steps

A few months after that tough talk with my dad, I was a fresh high school graduate and needed money for college. One afternoon, I was riding my bike and saw a sign outside of a UPS building that said they paid for tuition.

The company was smaller in those days but growing fast in Toronto. I had seen the professional uniforms the drivers wore and the clean brown delivery trucks. They made a positive impression on me, so I thought, *Why not?* I applied and was hired as a part-time employee, loading packages onto those trucks.

I worked the night shift, and that first night was a shock. It was late, chaotic, and fast-paced. I went home after clocking out and planned not to come back.

I wish I could say something grand inspired me to go back the second night. But I just happened to wake up right before my shift, and I really did need the money, so I went in.

As time went on, I came to understand the chaos and pace of the job were actually controlled aspects of a growing, evolving industry. The business was finding its legs in new territory. And I appreciated that. I wanted to be part of it.

Something else happened as I settled in. My hard work and outlook—driven by my dad's example and advice—were noticed. Until this point, I was just going with the flow and was content to let chance dictate my next steps. But my manager, a man named Michael Chabot, saw something in me that I hadn't seen in myself.

Michael didn't believe in leading from behind a desk and one night came over and said, "UPS is growing right now and there's a lot of opportunity. I think you can do some great things here." Michael then told me the UPS story of people starting part-time while going to school and how it can lead to bigger and better things. His observations and words of encouragement changed my life. From then on, he was my mentor.

UPS was growing, and there was a lot of opportunity. I was promoted to part-time supervisor and led a team of my own. I was young, and it was a challenge for sure, but I worked through it. And for the first time, I started imagining what could be possible with this company.

A couple of years later, I got to drive one of those sleek package cars I had admired and wear that professional uniform, which I came to know as a set of "browns."

From there, I took on bigger and bigger roles and started a family of my own. Along the way, I gained another UPS mentor named Glenn Rice. Like Michael, Glenn was a servant leader and his drive to achieve was second to none. Now I had two mentors cheering me on.

If I was unsure about the next move, Glenn would offer guidance. And if I hesitated, he would say, "What's the worst that could happen? You just might learn something."

He was the driving force behind me going back to school for a master's degree. He knew it would help my career, and it did. Michael and Glenn's mentorship was, and remains, a gift.

As UPS expanded its reach across international borders, I was tapped to lead business units in Europe and Asia. My job was to help these operations and their leaders achieve their full potential.

Such a pivotal role naturally came with its fair share of challenges. These units were not in Canada—where I had lived my entire life and spent my career—these were a world away. The cultures were new and unfamiliar. It was a learning curve and required a level of change management I hadn't even experienced, much less led, before that role. Not to mention the sacrifice my wife Sandy, and our sons Jacob and Fernando, were willing to make. Without their support, things would have been very different.

Recalling the lessons my dad, Michael, and Glenn taught me, I used visualization to chart the course to success. I was determined to solve any problems and remove obstacles because being a victim of circumstance was not an option. I had a clear vision of our destination, and it guided my actions.

Above all, I knew our people had to form the backbone of our accomplishments; otherwise, we'd never get where we needed to be. Success required transparency and a "we" mindset, along with a transition from *my* vision to *our* collective vision.

And we did it! We balanced cultural differences while preserving the essence of our business. It required some finesse, and it was a challenge. But the rewards were worth it. Those operations reached new heights and continue to support UPS's global success today. It was demanding but fulfilling work, and I consider what we accomplished a highlight of my career.

In addition to the amazing experience, I took away two key learnings:

First: There is no greater career support than a mentor.

Without Michael early on, I'm not sure I ever would've found my footing at UPS. Beyond the world-class training that UPS provided, he and Glenn gave me the confidence and leadership coaching that I needed to reach my potential.

Second: A vision built by one is nothing. A vision built by many is the future.

My vision of UPS's success in Europe and Asia was merely an aspiration until I had the support and buy-in of the local teams. Without their contributions and collaboration, my vision—*our* vision—wouldn't have come to life.

Paying It Forward

Once I'd had a taste of personal success, I wanted to help others imagine what was possible and visualize their own futures. So that's what I set out to do every day—uplift others who have the desire to grow.

Through this work, I've added another tenet to my leadership philosophy: pay it forward. In other words, remember the coaching and support you received and pass it on whenever you can. It's one of the ways I honor leaders like my dad, Michael, and Glenn. Some of my greatest accomplishments now come from paying it forward. It's rewarding to see people carve their own paths and create a great life here. And it's how I give back to the company that gave me everything I needed to thrive in the working world.

At UPS, our purpose is "moving our world forward by delivering what matters." For me, that means investing in our people and developing leaders who will imagine, visualize, and actualize our future. And it starts with just five lessons that I started learning many years ago:

Lead with empathy.

Dream big.

Find a mentor.

Embrace the power of collective vision.

Always pay it forward.

● ● ●

In the exercises that follow this chapter, you will begin by assessing your own success and defining or redefining what success means to you individually. First, let's spend some time with actress Rhys Olivia Cote, who shares more about her life as a child actress and model since the age of three.

Stories from the Heart

Rhys Olivia Cote—Success Comes at All Ages

From early on, my parents say I had the ability to draw people in and make them laugh. In fact, many of my earliest memories are of acting out mini stories for my parents and their friends. This love of acting feels like it's been there since the very beginning, and one day I dream of being onstage at the Oscars accepting an Academy Award for leading actress!

When I was three-and-a half, my parents entered me as a contestant in the cutest kids contest on the *Kelly & Michael Show* I placed in the top fifteen, and our local news station came to our house to do an interview. Soon after, I was signed by a modeling agency in New York City and Boston, and the work began. No one can understand the level of time and effort it requires to make this a career. At a very young age we traveled back and forth from our home in Maine to New York City and Boston, often treated as outsiders taking jobs away from local kids in the industry. Other parents were not welcoming most times, and we quickly learned to keep to ourselves. My mom persevered, thinking I had something special to share. I booked work with brands such as: OshKosh B'gosh, Pottery Barn Kids, American Girl Doll, and Nordstrom. I also worked for Oscar de la Renta many times and even opened up the designer's runway show in New York.

As time progressed, I added work for Ralph Lauren, Tommy Hilfiger Global, Love Shack Fancy, Laura Ashley, and numerous other global businesses. I added commercials to my café résumé, along with walking the runway and appearing on magazine covers and in the pages of different issues.

Just before I turned seven, my mom received a call from a producer, Kat Erangey, working on the TV show *Little Big Shots,* which was co-created and produced by Steve Harvey and Ellen DeGeneres. Ellen had seen some videos of me and asked my mom if I had a talent. We submitted a video of me as a "snail whisperer," and two weeks later I was in Los Angeles as the official Snail Whisperer from Maine. I appeared on the show one day before my birthday, and Mr. Harvey later gave me one of the biggest gifts I'd ever receive. He asked me if I knew what the "it factor" was. I had no idea. He went on to explain it was when a light shines from within—and that I had it. I knew then I not only wanted to act, I had to.

While in LA, a series of connections and meetings led to me acquiring an agent and manager—who have been supportive of my journey and are with me to this day.

I continued to model, but also went on auditions for TV shows and movies. I worked hard, came close, but nothing clicked until I was eight. I went into a casting call for *The Equalizer 2*, with Denzel Washington, and the casting director in LA plugged me into a more significant role. The director, Antoine Fuqua, made my dreams come true when I was invited to walk the premiere at the Grauman's Chinese Theater in LA. At this event, Denzel walked with me in his arms down the red carpet. It is a moment that I will never forget, and it made me more determined to build a career so that one day I would be the leading actress walking down the red carpet for my new premiere!

The industry is challenging and full of lessons. Through that, I've learned to cherish moments and the people I meet in every new experience. One of my fondest memories was when Denzel Washington's bodyguard, who told me to call him "Uncle Frank," shared that he'd seen quite a lot in his time working for Denzel, and he'd only met one other girl whose light shined like mine from within. He said it was Dakota Fanning! Uncle Frank and so many others granted me the support and inspiration to keep on going, because the business is fickle. Out of every thirty auditions, you may get a call back, a ping for a project and meet with casting and directors often, but booking a role is much harder. Sometimes, I would audition for a role only to find out later an already huge name got the job. My agent Meredith said it best to my mom like this: "She doesn't ever have to book. She always has great tapes and makes us look good. Honestly, beyond all of that, it's mind taffy and someone's choice. As long as she is having fun!"

People go into this thinking it's easy and that they can be famous. The truth is it's a lot of memorizing, hard work, and giving up time that you could be just being with your friends. It is dealing with constant let-downs and potential rejection. The public only sees the success and fame side of the story, but not how hard the person worked to get there.

The very best part about this industry has to be the people you meet. When actor Andrew G. Bennett was cast as my little brother in *Junkyard Dogs*, we began a lasting friendship that I treasure. While the work is long, arduous, and sporadic, I have learned how to become comfortable with both success and rejection, and that has been vital. I learned that sometimes I'm simply not the right fit, and until I get beyond a director session to signing paperwork, I know the job isn't yet mine. That has helped me become well-rounded, mature, and even more confident in my own ability. If I'm getting this far, I figure I must be doing something right.

Along with acting roles, I also continue to model. My latest print ad has been for Ralph Lauren, and you can find me on the cover of *Milan Weekly* in Italy. I have learned so much and am always still learning. I have found there are no short cuts to success. It comes with hard work and dedication. Overall, my experience has been positive and the people I have worked with have been understanding and kind. Every person involved in a movie, shoot, and ad is important, and that's something we all need to keep in mind.

I have been fortunate to go to a school where they work with me as I pursue my acting career. I have maintained high honors through junior high school, even as I have noticed it becoming more difficult socially. It isn't easy to make true friends, as some people seem to find my success unappealing. I don't let that weigh too heavily, however, and focus on the friends, sports, and activities that make me feel valued and supported.

I also love music and have been honored to sing at Carnegie Hall with other members of the Atlantic Harmonies Youth Choir, while I work on writing my own songs and attend a master class.

Strong, independent women keep me reaching for more, with a goal of one day securing a role as a regular in a TV series. I'm realistic in my future, and plan to study architectural engineering in college. Could all that change in the next four years? Perhaps, but for right now I feel comfortable in my goals.

Success requires hard work and a pliability to adjust if you fall. I would offer this advice: don't give up on your dreams, surround yourself with people who lift you up, make sure your team is working with you, and remember that we are all individuals. Don't try to question why someone else got the role you wanted, because honestly, there's more to it than you can imagine.

I feel very blessed to bring these stories to you. What did you learn? If you think about all of the things you dream about being or doing, is there one thing that comes to mind that you absolutely want to do? You don't have to answer this at this exact moment, that's okay.

I love to think about how success isn't just confined to one area of your life. I love to see people assess their lives and see where they need some work. So often we make a change and it ripples across other areas of our lives and helps us find the success we seek.

So, are you ready for your own assessment? On these next pages, you'll find heart-based exercises titled "Points to Ponder." There are two exercises at the end of each chapter, which create reflection points. In these first exercises, you can read a relaxation statement and then do the assessment. Please remember to be confident and kind to yourself, while remaining honest.

POINTS TO PONDER

Think. Write. Talk. Action. *(Because practice makes us our best.)*

EXERCISE 1: Let's Begin—Evaluating Success

To begin this exercise, I suggest reading this relaxation statement to help you focus and get in the frame of mind to take the assessment that follows.

RELAXATION TUNE-IN

Begin by taking several breaths. As you take a deep breath in and then out, imagine beautiful white light coming into your energy field from the top of your head down to your toes. Move your attention into your heart.

Feel love, a peace within your body begin to vibrate through your entire being. Taking another deep breath in and out, allow the energy of gratitude to emanate throughout your body—gratitude for everything in your life that has brought you to where you are today. Know that today you have the power of infinite possibilities for success within you. Take a deep breath, staying present in your heart center now.

Read this relaxation statement to yourself or out loud:

That's right! I now realize that I am very relaxed. In fact, the more I stop and take deep breaths, the more relaxed I feel. I am now aware that I am creating intentional success every day in every way. Each and every time I stop and take deep breaths, I am already going beyond my normal experience, which causes me to recognize my infinite possibilities. That's right! I now recognize that I am grateful for everything that has occurred in my life, which feels increasingly amazing. I now notice that my confidence has expanded exponentially. I am now ready to begin an honest assessment of my success today.

Let's take an honest assessment of how successful you feel in several areas of your life. In the areas noted below, please give yourself a score of 1 to 10 (with 1 being the lowest rating, and 10 being the highest). For each area, please place notes or comments to briefly explain your score.

Here's an example:

CAREER

Score: 5

Reason: I'm in my mid-forties and feel I need a career change so that I'm not commuting so much. I'm missing precious time with my family.

Before you begin, take a moment to get centered in your heart. (See Relaxation Tune-In above.) This is an exercise of love. Love yourself enough to give an honest evaluation of where you are in your life now. You may want to take a moment to read this relaxation statement once or twice. Focus your energy and think with your heart.

CAREER

Score: _____

Reason:_____

PERSONAL RELATIONSHIPS

Score: _____

Reason:_____

PROFESSIONAL RELATIONSHIPS

Score: _____

Reason:_____

EDUCATION

Score: _____

Reason:_____

VOLUNTEERING

Score: _____

Reason:_____

FINANCES

Score: _____

Reason:_____

HEALTH, NUTRITION, FITNESS

Score: _____

Reason:_____

OVERALL HAPPINESS, SENSE OF PEACE AND HARMONY

Score: _____

Reason:_____

SPIRITUALITY

Score: _____

Reason:_____

LIFESTYLE, HOME, AND LEISURE

Score: _____

Reason:_____

HABITS

Score: _____

Reason:_____

VACATION, HOBBIES, ACTIVITIES

Score: _____

Reason:_____

APPEARANCE

Score: _____

Reason:_____

OVERALL SUCCESS AND OUTLOOK ON LIFE

Score: _____

Reason:_____

EXERCISE 2: Journal Prompt—Vision and Defining Success

When I coach people personally and professionally, I encourage the use of a journal. In this book, we will have many journal prompts for the second exercise in each chapter. Remember, in your journal you can do *anything*. You can use crayons, markers, pens, or pencils. You can make drawings, or doodle. You can write long answers or bullet points. Do what resonates with you. You might not have all the answers or be able to provide specific details, and that is okay. Simply start somewhere and allow your mind, heart, and soul to think and grow. Let's start by answering these questions.

How do you define success?_____

_____

_____

_____

_____

_____

_____

Imagine you are already successful. What does a day in your life look like?

_____

_____

_____

Thinking of all the successful people that you know, who would you most like to emulate? Why? _____

_____

_____

_____

Those are big questions and I'm going to ask them again, so if you didn't answer them at this exact moment, don't worry, just keep moving forward. Let's continue.

CHAPTER 2
BELIEVE

In this Second Factor of Success, we believe. We believe in ourselves and have confidence; in turn, others believe and trust in us. We remove limitations to fully anchor in self-love, self-worth, gratitude, and self-confidence. In this factor, we take action to embolden the value of our unique self and establish a permanent, comprehensive confidence that is both internal and external. We can.

Team 153 is the most decorated team in the history of Georgetown University Baseball. Led by Head Coach Edwin Thompson, a native of Jay, Maine, the 153rd baseball team in Hoyas' history is unforgettable for many reasons.

SUCCESS TIP #8: Dream Big, Work Hard

With over 4,500 fans in attendance at the Big East Tournament at Prasco Park in Mason, Ohio, the team had its first-ever, post-season victory, back-to-back playoff appearances, and thirty-win season; most Big East and school wins in a two-year period; and all of the student-athletes carried a 3.2 GPA or higher. Ubaldo Lopez set a record for most home runs in school history. Our son's roommate and best friend, Jake Bloss, was named the Big East Pitcher of the Year and was ranked one of the top pitchers in the country. Jake was selected by the Houston Astros in the third round of the 2023 MLB Draft with the 99th overall selection. A right-handed pitcher from Greensboro, North Carolina, Jake became the highest draft pick in program history at 99th overall.

Beyond the accolades are drive, trust, adaptability, perseverance, and leadership. These five intangibles, which can't be measured, took Team 153 to new heights, and that is what everyone within earshot of this team could see and feel. As we huddled around our tailgates, all having had sons in baseball for many years now, we shared thoughts about the exceptional coaches, lifelong friendships made, and concern for those injured. Everyone connected to Team 153 believed in their confidence, success, and excellence.

While the Hoyas won thirty games, they also lost twenty-seven. Never did a parent, fan, coach, or member of the team speak negatively about an error, failure, or individual. They won as a team and lost as a team. Team 153 also battled injuries all season long. At one point, our son Cam (#33) referred to the group as a "walking hospital." But that "team first" motto held as teammates shifted positions to cover for others, and players supported each other during injury and recovery, making sure everyone was involved and present for the season as fully as possible.

In the 2023 Big East Championship, the Hoyas lost to UConn, knocked out Seton Hall, but then ultimately got eliminated from the tournament by ninth-ranked UConn. While understandably disappointed, the members of Team 153 could hold their heads high because they had accomplished so much.

SUCCESS TIP #9: Face Adversity with Confidence

A lefty pitcher for the Hoyas, our son Cam Guarino, #33, developed that throwing arm before he could walk and began to visualize becoming a baseball player as a child. With a passion for baseball from the very beginning, Cam was locked in on imagining his life in the game. However, life threw him a curveball.

This is from my journal on February 22, 2023:

It's 2:54 AM, and I'm wide awake, unable to sleep. I'm here in Myrtle Beach where my husband and I are taking a break from the Maine winter, heading south for several weeks to relax, take a breath, and watch Cam play. We're set up near the beaches and our view from the deck of our condo is of a rolling green golf course. We were so excited to watch Cam pitch as Georgetown traveled around North Carolina. Earlier that weekend in Cary, North Carolina, the Hoyas won their first series opener since 2012. I'd also scheduled a book signing for The Change Guidebook at the Myrtle Beach Barnes & Noble. Overall, we are feeling wonderful and grateful.

Back in the DC area, earlier today, as Cam took the mound against Navy, we couldn't help but reflect on the tumultuous year prior, filled with heartache, risk, determination, and a new beginning for him at Georgetown University. After two quick outs, all that hope for a remarkable baseball season quickly turned to horror when a line drive ripped off the bat on a direct trajectory for Cam's head. Miraculously, he threw up his pitching hand to take the brunt, sparing his face—but breaking or shattering his left hand. We thanked the angels or the stars or whatever deity assisted in preventing a catastrophic injury. It was what I would call a success upheaval. Life has changed in a moment.

He was pitching beautifully, too. Coach Edwin Thompson, in recapping the game, called Cam a "lefty specialist," who came in when the game was jammed up. Even as the ball screamed toward his head, Cam fielded it with his hand.

We were watching the live stats and saw a notification that stated: Hit back to pitcher. Then, nothing for over twenty minutes. Then the letter "I" appeared, which means just one thing:

INJURY. That awful feeling set in; our Cam was injured. We were frantic.

When the call finally came in, we learned Georgetown had beaten Navy 18-10 and Cam was in bad shape. "Are you okay?" we asked.

"No, I'm seriously injured. I'm certain I've broken, well, probably shattered, my left hand." We talked for a bit and then Cam boarded the bus back to Georgetown with doctor appointments scheduled for the next morning.

In all honesty, no one had any idea whether Cam would ever play baseball again. He called us later and sounded so sad and deflated.

At one point in worry-thinking, I praised all those who said focus on academics as you never know what will happen. That always caught our attention, and we reinforced it, so our son is obtaining his second master's degree while pitching at Georgetown. He has undergraduate and graduate degrees in environmental science, with honors, and just earned a 3.80 GPA at Georgetown where he is now studying sports management.

That information wasn't soothing or a silver lining at that moment, although we knew it would be at some point. I don't think anyone gets hurt like this and thinks, *Well, at least I have my master's degree.*

We knew the road ahead would be difficult. Cam was working through the injury, its impact on what could be his last year of baseball, and trying not to sink into devastation.

The fiction writer in me created tales of surgery. The science fiction writer in me wished to go back in time and reset the clock so that play, that pitch, that injury never happened.

I don't think anyone anywhere will tell you they haven't faced a situation they've needed to walk or run through with an exceptional attitude to get through it. How I wished we could turn back that moment and void out the pitch before it could happen. While we can't reset the clock on our lives, we can lock down our attitude and approach. In this case, it was an injury, but whatever the moment delivers, facing it with exceptional mindset control is essential. It may take all the strength you can muster, and the route may require a recalculation, but facing the obstacle often means charging at it full speed. That's exactly what we did here. It takes all the strength you can muster up to continue and especially if that means recalculating the route.

On that night after Cam's injury, I couldn't sleep. I closed the door and went to the kitchen to make myself some green tea and wrote in my journal. I recorded intense worry for Cam, and even when sleep did come, I prayed for him. *Please,* I begged, *let him get good news tomorrow.*

I also started to see success in a new light, and the possibility that it comes in strongest when all the cards are stacked against us and we're being pushed in a new direction.

I know life happens. Because of this happening, I am a mixture of mad, sad, and glad. Mad this happened, sad our son had to go through this, and glad it wasn't worse. Most of all, sadness ruled all the time—an overwhelming feeling that had me stuck for time to allow strength and positive energy to catch up and fuel healing and future success.

SUCCESS TIP #10: Believe in Yourself

It's easy to just tell you to remove limiting beliefs, ground yourself in self-confidence, and to not give your power away. Taking in that information and following through takes work and a strong belief in yourself— no matter what. To believe in yourself and to have confidence above and beyond what anybody else thinks is unconventional and against our natural instincts. You may need to adjust to keep yourself and your vision intact so as to not let others derail you or your dreams, vision, or goals. Here are more success tips and stories to create a solid foundation and practice for believing in yourself at all ages and stages.

It is here where I recommend investing in a great set of ear plugs and a whole lot of bubble wrap. Ear plugs to tune out naysayers, including yourself at times, and bubble wrap for the often-bumpy journey. Get tough! In the second factor of success, you believe in yourself no matter what and in spite of uncomfortable or imperfect circumstances.

If you've heard me speak or have been through my coaching classes, you've heard me talk boldly about the constant need to sidestep various types of people, but not trample on them or their feelings. Be polite. In general, keep the connection, don't burn the bridge, and firmly go where your own heart, truths, and energy take you.

It's *your* soul's calling, your vision, passion, or drive to do what makes you content and peaceful, not anyone else's. Take those ear plugs and bubble wrap and maintain your vision and open-mindedness. If you have kids or are in a role to teach or mentor children of any age, teach them to sidestep the naysayers and to believe in themselves. Teach them—and remind yourself—to never be a destroyer of dreams, visualization, imagination, or to block actions for anyone in their path. It's all hard enough without adding more obstacles. Not everyone has great measurables such as scores, talents, or analytics, however, you keep these people around, and on your team or in your circle, because they help others be their best. Don't dream crush and don't give up on your dreams.

SUCCESS TIP #11: Own Your Awesomeness

You are exceptional and it is time to own your awesomeness. Sift through the mediocre to find and keep the exceptional. Circumvent the mediocre.

You're very fortunate if you didn't grow up with a bad or negative parent, sibling, teacher, coach, neighbor, or friend; or, if you did, you found a way to sidestep them when needed. However, chances are, someone has tried to knock you down, make you feel less than or quit, and here's why: People behave relative to a collection of their own experiences being passed over to you. It's unfair, unkind, and can be downright cruel and twisted if intentional, but the sooner you realize that, the better you'll be.

It is precisely in this moment where, if you have even the slightest spark of passion and ambition for what it is you want to achieve, you must dig deep and drive forward and upward. If you don't see and stand firmly in your eventual success, even while in process, people generally can't see it or believe it, either.

SUCCESS TIP #12: Circumvent the Mediocre

As parents of four sons who are now in their twenties, we've witnessed so many wounded, negative people around our kids that we deemed them "the walking wounded." We discussed with the boys how some people are naysayers, don't have your best interest at heart, hurt others intentionally or unknowingly, and can amplify their own limiting beliefs, attitudes, jealousy, or unhealed wounds in ways to interfere with our ambitions. We reminded them that even friends can disguise themselves as walking wounded and shatter our self-confidence, vision, and success.

Sometimes, they can even *under-word* us, which can hurt, too. Words like underpaid, underestimated, underexposed, underachievement, under-valued, underutilized, understated, underrecognized, and so forth come to mind. We must resist the natural pull of these words to undermine our interests and throw us off track. When you sense someone exhibiting this behavior, move away. Engage differently or not at all. Understand that what you're seeing is a *them* problem, and don't make it a *you* problem.

Now, this can get complicated when that person is in a position of authority and has power over you; think a teacher, family member, coach, or boss. When we've encountered a coach like this, for instance, it can paralyze us with anger, worry, and fear. We've seen it on other parents dealing with an unscrupulous or narcissistic coach; when it involves your child, it burns like the heat of a hundred tropical suns. Yes, you may be stuck with this coach, or team, so don't underestimate the short- and long-term impact they can have on your family.

Here's an example: my husband and I were at a baseball game, sitting near the dugout, on a day when professional scouts turned out to watch the young talent. We overheard one of the coaches tell several of the scouts he had no one they'd be interested in. We were horrified. My husband and I felt strongly the coach had just negatively impacted highly gifted and talented baseball players in one short sentence. Who knows, was this coach slighted in the past by his own coach and merely carrying on his own trauma and disappointment? Perhaps. But, whatever the reason, it was awful to hear, sad to witness, and something we've never forgotten.

Don't be this person—ever. Foster growth and success in everyone you encounter. If a person has a vision for his own life, support it.

I think teachers, coaches, bosses, and leaders of all kinds are generally amazing. I've had way more great ones than suspect ones, but it remains those few sour apples in the group that we must learn to deal with. Pay very close attention to what your kids or spouse are sensing, and what your own heart is telling you, to avoid glossing over the walking wounded or failing to recognize their potential to terrorize.

As for teachers, I love so many of you, but across the board bad grades are a terrible reflection on your style. I don't see how anyone can ever fail a class or receive a D if there's been solid work and effort put in. I recall this one teacher, probably the most ornery math instructor I'd ever encountered, who took pride in telling us all about her prestigious degree and that she routinely handed out more D's and F's than A's. I believed that showed ineffective teaching, and our son was not learning at capacity in her class. In the moment, she was angry and defensive, but later called and informed me that upon reflection, she realized I was onto something. That teacher was brave enough to not only swallow criticism, but think on it, and adjust her style and attitude in a positive way. She became a better teacher because she had the decency and awareness to listen, react, and change. We all have that capacity and should probably use it more often.

As you have seen, to be blunt, I'm tired of people telling us consciously or unconsciously that we are all mediocre. Go around these people. Try to do it without drama and preserve the connection, as the people in question may change with time, healing, experience, and greater awareness.

SUCCESS TIP #13: Believe in the Underdogs

We often misdiagnose ourselves as being "under": underdogs who are undervalued and underappreciated. We may feel as though the odds are stacked against us, there is little chance of success or victory, and no one sees our value or potential because for whatever reason, we are not, nor will ever be, the odds-on favorite. Now, being the underdog has an emotional link to some of the most famous characters in cinematic history. Think *Rocky*, *Karate Kid*, and *Rudy*. They've made a mark in sports, too, from the US Olympic Hockey Team who gave us the Miracle on Ice, to New England Patriots' quarterback Tom Brady, who rose from the 199th pick in the NFL draft to be the greatest to ever play the game. I have felt like an underdog throughout my professional life, and I imagine you have, too. It's the gut punch of not being chosen, being belittled, ignored, or diminished. All of us have felt this at some moment, and our self-confidence has been torn to shreds. But therein lies the potential.

As a fellow underdog, my advice remains to give everything you have, even what's stored in your reserve tank. You may start at a disadvantage, with obstacles in every direction and at every turn, but motivation, faith, hope, and desire is willpower fuel, and that alone can remind you there is nothing left to lose. The paths we forge as underdogs are often the ones that are bumpier, more difficult to navigate, but are illuminated from within even during our darkest hours.

Jesse and Emily Cole, The Savannah Bananas, and Georgetown Baseball's Team 153 were all considered underdogs. They had to battle through adversity and hope that the lucky stars would align for them. In my life, timing and my personality have brought me to many other underdogs, and I cheer wholeheartedly for their success. In fact, I have a tender spot for them, and tend to throw my energy behind each one. Underdogs take success and define, redefine, format, and deliver their own unique brand of it. Wins, when they come, are then so deeply appreciated; seeking more becomes a mantra, then a pattern, and finally, a lifestyle, and leadership!

If you're a perennial underdog, keep this in mind: believe in yourself, search for and then surround yourself with others who support you, and be ready to work. Underdogs already know nothing is handed to them, so be persistent and resilient. Earn it. Believe in yourself and everything you dream of being and doing.

SUCCESS TIP #14: Surround Yourself with Awesomeness

Over the years, there have been coaches who have been instrumental in our son's college baseball career and sport mentality. We are even honored and proud to call a bunch of those coaches family and are very grateful for their incredible wealth of knowledge and expertise. Great coaches have a knack for spotting talented athletes and diamonds in the rough and developing their talents while keeping their attitudes realistic and balanced for each individual. They also help keep parents accurately informed as to their child's current abilities and provide constructive, honest feedback for their growth.

One of our favorites, a retired coach, would talk about some very interesting and mostly challenging situations where he helped families and baseball players at all levels. Sometimes, he would talk about how he could easily identify less-than-stellar coaching and even help extract kids from some less-than-outstanding situations.

My husband, son, and I would listen intently because the stories were interesting and ones where you are rooting for a person's success, where circumstances need to be overcome. The one thing that we didn't fully expect was that our son would find himself in this kind of situation. So, when our son's college baseball experience began to sour, we reached quickly for expertise.

SUCCESS TIP #15: You Can Be as Good as You Think You Are

Our son Cam was in his last year playing baseball at Division II University of New Haven. Although he had been offered a sixth year due to COVID-19 extending eligibility, and even a scholarship to return, he felt undervalued in multiple ways. He felt demoralized and was losing his love for baseball. He had maintained a 3.90 GPA, graduating magna cum laude, and won the first-ever Presidential Award for Academics. He was one class away from his master's degree in environmental science when he began discussing a plan to make the best of his final year there. Ultimately, Cam determined that it would be best to transfer away from the problem and formed a plan for him to transfer and develop his skills as a pitcher.

For the summer of 2022, Cam pitched in The Old North State League, a prestigious college summer league in North Carolina. His head coach was Rob Shore, and the league owner was Alec Allred, who would both further support Cam's development. Our son moved to North Carolina and lived with Ms. Linda Pritchett and her two sons, who were an outstanding and supportive host family. He worked intensely to develop his pitching skills and went to the Wake Forest Pitching Lab for evaluation. In addition to the physical success, Cam worked to restore his confidence and mental toughness. By the end of the summer, Cam had gone 4–0 in his summer league, with an ERA of 2.19 and 50 strikeouts in 41 innings.

This success was quickly recognized as Cam began to get offers to transfer and ultimately transferred to Georgetown University with beloved Head Coach Edwin Thompson, who has twenty years of experience coaching at all different levels of college baseball. He and Cam teamed up to bring you these next stories about believing in yourself.

Stories from the Heart

Coach Edwin Thompson—Dream Big

Failure and adversity crush dreams and steal opportunity. But it doesn't have to be this way. This is how I used both failure and adversity to build the life of my dreams. It wasn't easy and I didn't even know it was happening until much later, but on reflection, I took setbacks and transformed them into power moves.

It starts with motivation. Leading others is a passion of mine, but I've only become good at it—practiced and confident—by failing first. I would stray off track often when I was growing up, dreaming the day away in school, my dad often telling me, "No stinking thinking," when I'd boot up motivational cassette tapes on long car rides. At the time, I wasn't even sure what all of that meant, only that I was desperate to harness my dreams for the future into a plan of action. As I now look back upon nineteen years of coaching college baseball, and the groundwork of my approach laid so long ago, I turned distraction to focus to reveal an ability to build connections with players that remains my signature trait. You see, leadership is functional, with limitless potential to develop throughout your life once you know how to let it fly.

The best sort of leadership grows from disappointment and, yes, pain. It grows stronger beneath a callus and hardens into a more resolute resolve. I remember being cut from my junior high baseball team and immediately throwing out excuses to remove fault from myself. It was a mistake, I railed. I was overlooked! My dad listened to my version of being snubbed, but not for long. When I was done whining, he asked me a bold yet simple question. "Did you prepare like you could have?" I thought about that. "Son, you can make excuses or make things happen." It was plainly spoken but hit hard. I realized at that moment how much more I could have done to prepare myself for try-outs. My dad's message lit a fire in me like never before. I promised myself I would do whatever it took to never get cut from a team again. The lesson sits with me to this day: if you want anything in life, earn it.

Growing up as I did in Maine, the weather was less than ideal for a kid who wanted to play in the major leagues. But this newfound spark forced me to figure out how to work harder and better to find a path to my goals. I credit both my parents for displaying a day-to-day work ethic in a small mill town that centered around family and responsibilities. I learned from them how to push through losses, to never rise too high from the wins, and maintain a steady dedication to becoming a version of myself they'd be proud of.

Those growing-up years in Maine planted the philosophy I have taken with me to the dugouts of high-level college programs. Have compassion but be tough. Excuses get in the way of balance; balance is primary to steadiness; steadiness leads to success. Just like my dad taught me, I take myself seriously enough to impart confidence in my coaching, but not too seriously as to become unrelatable to my players. They know I am as human as they are, imperfect, but always honest. Once I was able to connect with them, and my players trusted me, we grounded ourselves in that shared brand of humility. Then, the group—players and staff—could move seamlessly in a chosen, almost predetermined direction together as one.

Does it happen right away? Not necessarily, and that hard truth hit during my first head coaching job at Bates College in Lewiston, Maine. I was twenty-eight years old, and far from ready to be a head coach. The program also needed a punch of confidence after years of posting a mediocre record that continued through my first year with the team. Collectively, we needed a shift. It began on the very first day of my second year. I looked out at the hopeful faces of my players and recited three words: "Hold the rope." I could see confusion spread, as I imagined them pondering what exactly that meant. Gathering the team into a circle, I showed them a big rope. "Everyone here has a responsibility to do our part to help the team win," I explained. All eyes were focused on me as this visual representation of all hands pulling the rope toward victory took hold. Turns out, it helped connect a hungry and talented group of players to the fortitude they needed to leap ahead of 138 previous teams and set a new school record for wins that season.

In September of 2020, right in the throes of the COVID-19 pandemic, I was hired to lead the Georgetown University Division 1 baseball program. Typically, once a new hire is announced there's a press conference and an event on campus to introduce the new coach and team. But the norm was twisted into new protocols we all had to follow, so my first meeting with the team was held over Zoom, and we'd continue that way for the next six-and-a-half months. With students no longer living, studying, working out, and practicing together due to the virus, the next big challenge was to figure out how to make them a team over computer screens. I loaded up my dad's reminder when I'd failed to secure a spot on that long-ago baseball team: make excuses or make things happen. I was determined to pull this team together, show them who I was as a person and a coach, and set the right tone during an unparalleled public health emergency that had closed our school and so many others across the country.

By March 7, 2021, we learned we would indeed have a season. We went on to produce a 6 and 25 record, and no fairy-tale ending. But I, and the team, realized through the hardships and challenges that we had worked through something special together, and once we based the entire season in gratitude to have had the opportunity to play, that seemed so much larger than the losses we'd accumulated.

What that first year taught us all was how priorities and timing could work in our advantage. Waking up with thanks in our hearts to do the very thing we'd all grown up loving showed me as a new coach how vital the right mindset and process would be for wherever my career took me. The game may be the same, yet the circumstances have been as fluid as the wind. I had to hold strong to everything I'd learned to now teach, model, and motivate the impressionable young players in my care.

There is no secret to the process of what it takes to win in whatever you are doing. The formula comes with equal parts humility, gratitude, and confidence that grows from both success and failure. Believe in what you are doing and the process that got you there. Set goals but make habits equal so one leads to the next. Dream big but work bigger, listen to those wiser than you, and believe that one day, you'll get to places you never imagined you'd see.

Stories from the Heart

Cam Guarino—Believing in Myself

I was a fall 2022 graduate transfer recruit for Team 153—the baseball team at Georgetown University. This experience with the Hoyas helped me understand how to truly believe in myself.

I had to make a very hard decision to transfer from a place I had been at for five years to a completely new environment that would test my resolve every step of the way. I just want to start out by saying that change is very hard to make, as readers of my mom's work are well aware of, but you can work toward success by being present and focused on where you are in your journey and where you wish to go. Being truthful to yourself is important as it allows you to gauge where you are and assess your perception of yourself, but you must also be able to understand what it is you are working toward. If you were already at the level you want to be, you would already have achieved your goal. The NCAA D1 baseball transfer portal is where I learned how to perceive myself and work toward a goal that I used to think was impossible.

In May 2022, with a few classes left to finish my master's degree, I entered the transfer portal for baseball. While COVID had many challenges, one benefit was the extra eligibility it offered me. I decided to pursue my dream of attending Georgetown and playing baseball. It took a series of moves to ultimately receive the offer from Coach Thompson. The first was to enter the transfer portal, which is an incredibly frightening place to be as a student-athlete because you must leave your current school with no guarantees that another offer to play will come. I also needed to play summer baseball during my time in the portal in an area where coaches could see me easily, which is why I moved to North Carolina from Maine, to live with a host family and play for the High Point Hushpuppies.

In the transfer portal, I had to be prepared for any situation and be mentally ready to put myself out there to schools to show who I am as a person, while also performing as best as I can on the field. I also took on an internship so that my prospects for graduate school would be better. I interned at the High Point Rockers, a minor league baseball team, as their home field was where my summer team was playing. I had very little experience working at the front office for a sports team, but I had an idea of what is needed from my five years of college baseball experience. This was the start of me realizing that I could accomplish goals that I had thought were impossible, because I had begun to believe that I was not good enough or experienced enough. I had to sidestep myself. With this, I decided that my goal was to play my final year of college baseball at Georgetown, while getting the best education possible to position me for a future in sports. My Plan A was in motion.

As I have proceeded further along my athletic career, I have found myself increasingly drawn to coaching, teaching, and leading. My baseball experiences, insights, and pools of knowledge are growing each year as I learn from each season of play. I continue to learn from my mentors, certain coaches, and teammates I have met along the way, which has further solidified my desire to be involved in baseball in any way I can. I hope to be able to play for as long as possible and achieve the goals that I set for myself when I was younger.

As my career has developed, I have found that a lot more hard work is ahead of me to get to those places with my athletic ability, but I look forward to those challenges and opportunities. The amazing part about sports is that you can be involved in ways beyond what you can do on the field. This is what I hope to be able to do in life, which is to be involved in baseball for as long as I can and share my experiences with those that are eager to learn. Whenever it is time to put down the baseball and pick up a briefcase, I feel I will be equipped.

It is my goal to be able to bring my background, experiences, and network of people to demonstrate my unique perspective on baseball. My objective is to not only learn as much from others, but also collaborate and share my student-athlete experiences to give a broader understanding of the many distinct aspects of student-athlete life. I have been told by many of my coaches and teammates that my knowledge of the game of baseball is vast and that I am a true student of the game. I lead by example every day by showing what work is needed to perform well on the field. Most of that work is through physical preparation by fueling the body correctly, hydrating, stretching, post-work treatment, and mental preparation.

The most important of all, however, is the energy, effort, and execution you put into your work. Those are some of the only things that a person can control; whatever happens in life is decided by what energy is put in, having a positive or negative mindset, and the actions leading up to the game; effort, which is the ability to stay focused on the job at hand, eliminating distractions, and being able to adapt to changing situations; and execution, which is getting a job done as best as possible under the circumstances. After bad games, it is not about what happened. It's not about beating yourself or blaming others. It is about how one prepares oneself for the next task and how to overcome adversity. The greatest opponent and critic of an athlete is always the athlete themselves. Limiting the mental intrusions of doubt and being able to see the broader perspective of performance, is crucial to being great on and off the field.

These are some of the things I have learned over my athletic career, and I apply them to every aspect in my life. What I have learned can help others, even if they are not athletes, and this is what I hope to be able to impart on those around me: to show people to take a step back and reevaluate or reassess their situation. I had to take a step back and reassess my life after my fifth year at New Haven; it was a very hard thing to do, but it was crucial for me to see what I want to do in life. Creating change is a very scary thing to do, but I did so with a growth mindset and goals that I set out to achieve. Finishing my final year of NCAA eligibility at Georgetown was one of my most important goals.

During my first appearance pitching for Georgetown against Navy, my pitching hand was fractured after a line drive "comebacker" hit me. This was the last season of college baseball that I would play, and I was devastated. I said partial goodbyes to most of my teammates, as I thought there was no way to recover from this injury in time for the remainder of the season. I thought my hand was shattered.

Although it was awful to have an injury to my pitching hand, I'm thankful it wasn't worse and that I wasn't seriously injured, as the line drive was over 105 mph. However, in those moments that followed the injury, I coped with deep sorrow.

One of the best surgeons in the Washington, DC, area would operate on me to insert a pin in the palm of my left hand a bit under my pinky finger. Prior to this, we had met on a conference call, and I was relieved by his calm assurance that he would take great care of me, and I'd be back up pitching again during the season.

Thanks to Dr. Curtis Henn and the Baseball Gods, soon after a successful surgery and rehab, I was cleared to pitch again. I pitched in three games. It wasn't perfect, but I was back out there on the mound and at peace, having achieved my second goal—to pitch for Team 153 again.

I'll wind this up by saying that you can be as good as you think you are. Don't let anyone tell you differently. Had I listened to coaches telling me things about myself that I didn't believe I would have quit long ago and for sure after that fifth season at New Haven.

Go into the world where people believe in you and care about you. Find people who help you believe in yourself and help you reach your potential, so that you, in turn, master how to help others.

The pin in my left hand will always be a reminder to be grateful and to believe in myself!

POINTS TO PONDER

Think. Write. Talk. Action. *(Because practice makes us our best.)*

EXERCISE 3: Choose One Area

This exercise is designed for you to have more success. In your success assessment in Exercise 1, you scored yourself from 1–10 in several areas. Now please identify four areas from that exercise where you scored the lowest. Write them in your journal or below. You will select one of these areas to work on.

1. Area: _____ Score:_____

2. Area: _____ Score:_____

3. Area: _____ Score:_____

4. Area: _____ Score:_____

To help you get more clarity, consider reviewing what you've written above and then close your eyes. Take a few deep breaths and bring one of the areas you listed into your vision. Take a deep breath and ask your heart, *Is this the most important area to work on?*

Repeat this process for each area on your list.

Next, take another deep breath, staying present with your heart-based thinking. You are ready to choose. Of these four areas, which one would you most like to focus on so that you can expand and create more success?

Write it here:_____

_____

_____

_____

_____

Next, since we love action, we are going to put our words in motion and create space to grow, change, and have the incredible success we crave. Please complete the following exercise.

Area: _____(from Exercise 3)

I choose to focus on _____ (area).

What do you currently believe about this area?

_____

_____

What new beliefs do you think would help you to expand in this area?

_____

_____

To obtain this success, I realize I need to take action to support my new beliefs. Here are two goals and actions I am willing to take:

Goal:_____

_____

Action:_____

_____

Date: _____

Signature: _____

Goal:_____

_____

Action:_____

_____

Date: _____

Signature: _____

I have always dreamed of _____

_____

_____

_____

I dream this because I _____

_____

_____

_____

When I imagine I have realized my dreams, I feel _____

_____

and my success looks like _____

_____

_____

To reach these actions I need to keep thinking _____

_____ and _____

_____

I need ear plugs and bubble wrap for the following situations and people:

_____

_____

_____

I am going to take this action to work around these situations and people:

_____

_____

_____

That's right, I am _____and I am _____

That's right, I allow _____and I also allow_____

That's right, I create _____ and I create _____

I am loved. I am successful. I am joy. I create harmony and peace.

I am clear with my vision, purpose, and belief in myself. I surround myself with those who have my best interests at heart. I follow through in my intentions.

I am_____(your name)

EXERCISE 4: Journal Prompt—Defining Success

Remember, in your journal, you can do ANYTHING. Use crayons, markers, drawings, writing, doodles, short answers. You might not have all the answers and details to these questions. It is important to start somewhere and allow your mind, heart, and soul to think and grow. Let's answer these questions.

Dream big! What are you dreaming of accomplishing?

_____

_____

_____

_____

_____

_____

What or who has stopped you from achieving this dream?

_____

_____

_____

_____

_____

Are you achieving your dream and need to sustain the momentum of success?

_____

_____

_____

_____

_____

CHAPTER 3
FOCUS

In the Third Factor of Success, we focus. We focus on what it takes to accomplish our big dreams and goals. We focus on our vision for ourselves, our passion, and happiness. We follow our dreams and goals. We work when nobody else is working. We go above and beyond. Here, we learn how to thrive within that elusive state of mind that supports passion, happiness, and an attainable mission. We calm the chaos by learning to manage our energy. We focus our energy by centering and grounding ourselves in self-love, self-worth, and gratitude.

Emily Francis and her family were living in a small town in Georgia before they sold practically everything they owned, packed up what was left, and moved in pursuit of a new life on the Mediterranean island of Malta. Prior to that move, Emily felt stifled in her daily life and had a constant nagging pull toward something more that would feed her own free-spirited nature, as well as her family, in a more complete way. Life in that small Southern town was not a good fit for her or her family. When you don't feel safe or supported in your environment, trying to fit into a space that was never meant for you can cause a level of stress that can wreak havoc on your emotional and physical health. Nothing about life in that town felt healthy or safe to her. She practiced finding peace amidst the chaos, but it was not enough.

To exist in a way that finds you constantly wishing for a different life is not a way to live at all. It's a life of coasting in neutral instead of exploring and feeling energized by the environment around you. It can be difficult to maintain focus when things don't line up with who you are and what you want for your life. If you aren't happy, as Emily wasn't, the world can start to feel very small. The two most important things she wanted for her family were not accessible where she was. Those two things were: 1) a GMO-free country where foods were not sprayed with harmful, poisonous chemicals; and 2) a place where children did not have to practice active shooter drills in their schools. Living in a safe country with tight gun control was particularly important. Malta checked both of her boxes. That was the driving force in the family's collective decision to follow their instincts and create a new life for themselves: getting to a place where they felt safe and supported. From there, finding freedom in the world around her, she was able to create an entirely new life and career for herself, one that creatively nourishes every part of her, one that was hard-earned and entirely deserved. This is where focus, hard work, and consistency pay off in spades.

In 2020, Emily A. Francis, her family (including four animals) picked up and moved across the ocean to a destination they had never so much as visited and created an entirely new life for themselves on the tiny island of Malta. Her husband's company made this move possible, and she took the opportunity to completely change course and focus on her own career. For the last twenty years, she has been an author and a clinical bodyworker, writing books on body healing.

With incredible determination in a brand-new place, Emily had to figure out what else inspired her and then focus on finding a way to go do it. She began writing for the local tourism magazine, *Oh My Malta!* and now writes a regular column titled "Emily in Malta" that follows the local foods as they come into their season. These articles are not only for their online and print magazine, but they are also filmed with a camera crew. Emily has grown to do live, in-person interviews with local farmers, fishermen, and chefs about the way foods are grown and harvested.

Malta has a full ban on GMO foods, and this was something Emily was extremely passionate about. Figuring out how to find these farmers, then asking to go to their homes, as well as dealing with language barriers and putting them on camera required a level of tenacity that she had never had to draw upon before.

Emily adds, "It is nearly impossible to accomplish anything through the telephone here as English is the second language behind Maltese. People don't understand my American accent over the telephone and e-mails are not used as much as you would imagine they would be. Phones don't even have voicemails here. The most difficult part was finding the farmers to speak with from the start. The stories I could tell in finding each person to interview are hilarious! I began from zero and introduced myself one by one to any farmer or fisherman I could find and built my reputation with each one of them as I went along."

Emily shares that these experiences have taught her so much about success and the steps needed to get there. She says, "Applying focus and helping me learn has made me so much more resourceful. It has also made me profoundly more cognizant of understanding what it truly means to eat locally, seasonally, and mindfully."

Emily has gone on to add another bestselling book to her credit, *The Taste of Joy: Mediterranean Wisdom for a Life Worth Savoring.* Emily tells me that what she has learned from these farmers, and using food as a metaphor for life has helped her imagine what is possible, how to believe in herself, and focus on what it takes to accomplish her dreams and goals.

Emily's efforts have been magnified in cause and effect. She has remained focused and continues to show up; this propels her forward toward the rewards. She's "in" with the locals and the bookstores all carry her new book in their front window displays. Note that this didn't happen until she went to each one and asked for them to add it!

She says she takes nothing for granted and continues to foster her relationships with families long after she and her crew have come and gone with the cameras.

Emily says, "They have become sacred friends of mine, and they feel the same about me. The magazine and I hosted a public festival this year to celebrate the new book and many of my farmers came and sold their local products that I discuss in the book. It has been a tremendous circle of give-and-take between us and continues to be this way. The way that locals love here in many ways is through food; it is their love language. I have become part of this language and culture."

SUCCESS TIP #16: Align Your Heart, Truths, and Energy

Like Cam Guarino in the last chapter, Emily had to focus and course correct to align everything for her best success. What a move and story!

In *The Change Guidebook*, I guide readers to think with their heart, live and show up authentically, and understand that you go where you place your energy. I believe that when these things align, you can do anything. I also believe you must do these things with a firm understanding that you aren't entitled to time, and that nearly everything revolves around our ability to manage our time and also how we navigate. We have a choice in every moment of how to be. You have choices in what you say, what you do, how you react, and more. My goal as a coach and creator of The Best Ever You Network is to help people live their lives with love, joy, confidence, self-worth, success, peace, gratitude, and abundance with momentum and positive energy. You have a choice to be your best in each moment of your life. Saying this and doing this might feel like worlds apart. Here are some more success tips to get you started.

SUCCESS TIP #17: Do the Opposite

In those moments, remember, as someone is ticking another is tocking; as someone is zigging another is zagging. Be yourself. So often this means we are grinding against the norm, the crowd, the popular, what is standard, what has always been, the way it has always been done—and on and on and on. There is a saying on my refrigerator, one that I raised my kids on. It says, "Don't follow the masses, for sometimes the M is silent." The saying often screams "Do the opposite!"

In practical terms and using this in your life, it goes like this:

If everyone around you is doing something, do the opposite or something else.

For example:

> If your values are to remain sober, you may not go to a party where there is drinking. You might opt for a movie instead. However, if you are at the party and everyone starts drinking, you have a choice in every moment at the party to do the opposite. Fill your glass with water or soda or a non-alcohol choice if available. Bluntly put, if everyone is doing the same thing, don't.

I get letters from people annoyed by this concept. However, I can assure you this practice, which might take practice on your part, is something I have been doing since around eighth grade and it has served me so well over the years. We've taught it to our sons, and it has saved them from some situations where others didn't fare so well.

Can you think of an instance where you went with the crowd despite your inner voice telling you not to?

SUCCESS TIP #18: Practice Comprehensive, Well-Rounded Success

I'm a huge fan of well-rounded, comprehensive success. This means you assess each area of your life and feel a sense of success and peace as you reflect. Often, we see people with wild, "world-class" success in one area, for instance their career or business, yet they are seemingly miserable or unable to get it together in their personal relationships, or they struggle with substance abuse or other problems. Often, those who strongly succeed in one area focus only in that area, to the detriment of other parts of their lives. When this happens, we are often served with a jarring wake-up call for us to make the necessary changes.

On the contrary, when you practice comprehensive, well-rounded success, it creates the depth needed to focus on multiple areas, making success and all its facets work for you. It's the daily seemingly little things that we often take for granted that help us be our best, most successful selves. There are world-class behaviors and principles that you can apply to your everyday, "ordinary" life to make it *extraordinary*. That said, I'm also a huge fan of taking a skill or talent and nurturing and developing it to help a person reach world-class success and excellence.

In either case, it is important to not only imagine and believe, but now also focus. There is a lot to do between imagining and envisioning our success and *actualizing* success! You've got to start taking action to move toward actualization.

SUCCESS TIP #19: Focus and Do the Work

According to Cal Newport, MIT-trained computer science professor at Georgetown University and *New York Times* bestselling author of the book *Deep Work*, we get all we can get from ourselves when we do things without distractions and push our thinking to the limits. With this type of work, which is called "deep work," we acquire values and skills that are authentic to us. "Shallow work," on the other hand, is doing things that don't require our highest focus. We typically do these things while distracted. Cal goes on to say that deep work is becoming rare in this age of distraction and is also becoming more valuable. He suggests those who work deep will reap rewards beyond those who don't.

Reading this book made me think about a surgeon performing heart surgery who stops every ten minutes to check his e-mail and text messages. Scary, right? Now, I know that would never happen . . . right? It makes me think of how distracted we can be, how our habits and behaviors serve or don't serve us, and how we can also numb ourselves with a variety of things when we need to heal instead.

I think meetings, phone calls gone wild and unstructured, as well as e-mails, including that dreaded "reply-all" function, are modern-day massive wastes of time. The solution relies on intention. Slow down, place boundaries where they're needed, and align your mind with your highest priorities: the items that drive your thoughts and ambition. This will guide you to the clarity and focus to do the work necessary for success.

SUCCESS TIP #20: Manage Your Time

If we aren't entitled to time, then it's high time we learn to focus on what matters to us and eliminate anything that doesn't support our success. Yes, I'm suggesting you stop doing things that don't serve your best interests. Allow me to introduce you to the five D's: Distractions, Destructors, Deductors, Derailers, and Drama. The five D's are time and energy wasters. The good news is the repellent is in your full control and the dosage and usage.

Distractions **prevent you from giving your full attention in that moment.**

Destructors **tear down or deallocate something you've built and pull you out of scope, perhaps even altering you or your perspective.**

Deductors **take away from your life. They subtract.**

Derailers **completely take you off course. They thus halt progress.**

Drama **creates a spectacle with unexpected events, twists, and turns.**

We want to minimize and control the five D's in our lives by first understanding them and then learning to manage them in our lives. The opposite, which are the A's, help fight the five D's.

So next let's look at the A's. These are lighter and more angelic in appearance. They add or contribute to your life and honor you in every way. The good news is you get to choose your A's. Take a look at the twelve A's:

Awesomeness

Awareness

Abundance

Action

Allow

Authenticity

Align

Assess

Acceptance

Attention

Actualize

Amplify

By no means are those the only A words you can use. These are the ones I suggest to get you started. We will do more with our A words in the exercises that follow at the end of the chapter. For now, please look at the list and circle the one that you feel you wish to focus on the most.

Write it here: _____

Why did you choose this word? _____

_____

_____

SUCCESS TIP #21: Control the Controllables

Are you one of those people who feels like they take one step ahead and then several steps back? I don't know about you, but life to me often feels like we are trying to find a cure for chaos. The other day, my husband and I cleaned our house and everything was just looking great. No sooner had we finished and sat down when the cat puked all over the couch after eating the flowers I had put on the kitchen counter. Fifteen minutes later, the dog came in from outside and tracked mud up the stairs. Later that same day, our son lost his wallet. To top it all off, a storm blew through the next day, toppling a tree in the yard.

Ever have a day or a string of days or even several years that feel like that? Perspective is key here, as these things mentioned certainly qualify for any of the five D's for sure. However, life happens. As a master life coach for over fifteen years, here are some of the most common phrases I have heard from clients:

Why did this happen?

My life sucks.

I don't have good luck.

I am not successful.

Why me?

I can't . . . because . . .

I don't know how . . .

Why does this keep happening (to me)?

What can I do?

Is it me?

What am I doing wrong?

I don't know what to do.

I don't know how to get through this.

If they would have . . . then I . . .

This is just awful.

I can't manage.

And so forth. You get the idea. Here are some solutions.

SUCCESS TIP #22: Get Perspective

Life happens, I totally understand. The long-term effect of even one moment can transform your life for the better or worse. Some moments call for everything you've got in you to handle the situation and prevail. When you encounter something that totally disrupts your normal way of life, or when things seemingly come out of nowhere and derail your safety, security, life as you are living it, well-being, and so forth, it is life-altering. This is a reminder that we can't always control what happens, so we need to control what we *are* able to while also realizing that not everything is soul-crushing. Our dog's muddy feet on the carpet are not going to cause the world to end or alter our lives significantly. So, it isn't as crazy as it feels in that moment compared to what other people are facing. Get and maintain perspective.

SUCCESS TIP #23: Create a No-Drama Zone

Ever been around someone whose life is just one thing after another after another after another and you just want off their life roller coaster? You want to move forward without their unexpected twists and turns. They feel like the person who just can't, no matter what, get their shit together. Whether they never have enough money or have trouble at work—whatever it is—it is a never-ending series of problems. It is almost like they feed on the discord and can't find true peace, but they are unaware of the energy they are wasting. How do we insulate ourselves from their drama and yet be helpful if needed? Here are some ideas using the "lob" method. This means that whatever the drama or current crisis is, you are there, but you are lobbing it back to their court, like a tennis volley. The responsibility rests within them to learn how to curtail their drama and you don't necessarily need to get sucked in.

L—Listen: Quietly listen. Don't offer advice or say anything in response. If you need to respond, lob it back to them in the form of a question, such as "Well, what do you think?"
O—Observe: Quietly watch. Consider just stepping back to observe this person who might be a friend, coworker, or family member. You set the time frame. It could be a day or could be a month. You have the choice to observe and choose whether or not you wish to continue to be around them.
B—Be: Be there for them, but it doesn't mean you have to solve their day-in and day-out drama. Don't loan them money, for example. Remember, with drama-zone types, when one drama resolves, another is usually close behind.

Let's meet our next contributor, Michael McGlone. Michael is a superstar who lights up the world not only with his many artistic gifts, but also with his love and sincerity. A brilliant writer, musician, actor, songwriter, and comedian, he is someone who has said, "I am blessed to be doing everything with my life I was born to do." Whether in movies like *The*

Fitzgerald Family Christmas, The Brothers McMullen, The Bone Collector, and *She's the One,* or on TV as *Person of Interest*'s Detective Szymanski or Dennis Lang on *NCIS: Hawai'i,* his work as an actor is an unrelenting display of natural talent. His comedy, his music, his spot-on Christopher Walken impression and Geico commercials have been entertaining us for years, though it's his desire to connect with, inspire, and love others that I've found equally memorable.

For me, he is one of those famous people of whom it can be said a professional success is matched by a very personal one, typified by his often witnessed and vibrant ability to make others feel like a star.

Michael says, "What's best for others is what's best for me." This is a truth he lives by, which you will see abundantly illustrated in the piece below.

Stories from the Heart

Michael McGlone–The Greatest Success

The greatest success to me is self-love, as it is only through that that one is able to most fully love others and have peace in their lives. Without an appreciation of yourself as fundamentally deserving of love, it will always be impossible to relate to yourself or anyone else in a consistently healthy way and have the enriching life you deserve. When you are centered in knowing your value, it very naturally follows you see the same in others. In the abundance of this positive vibration, you have the greatest space to express your unique excellence and beauty to the world and encourage others to do the same.

In the past, my idea of the greatest success was different; it had less to do with self-love than it did with what people commonly pursue to achieve a kind of love, or to compensate for the lack of it: professional accomplishment, money, and fame. To a degree, I achieved all of these things early in my career as an actor and it was through the achievement of this kind of success that I found myself, ironically, failing. And it is that story I want to share with you.

In my early twenties, I was gifted with a film, one that would result in me establishing a career as an actor, which was the reason I came to New York City in 1993. When I say "gifted" I don't mean it was flatly given to me; I did audition for it, though I will forever see it as a divine blessing because it was so perfectly suited to me. That film was

The Brothers McMullen, and I got it having serendipitously responded to an ad in the actor's trade newspaper, *Backstage*. It still exists as a printed publication today, with a very successful online presence as well, though at this time it was only available as a hard copy paper that came out every Wednesday.

There were always various jobs listed, and one day there was an ad for a film called *The McMullen Brothers* (later, the name would be slightly adjusted to *The Brothers McMullen*). The ad listed a brief description of the story and the three Irish-American brothers it centered around, all with different personality types and at different places in their lives. I thought, based on my last name alone, I should get an audition. So, I submitted a headshot, stapled to my most professionally presented résumé (which featured only non-professional jobs), and after weeks of waiting: nothing. I felt very put off by that. Who did these people think they were? Then I got a phone call, resulting in me meeting someone who has been as important as anyone to my career as an actor—Eddie Burns.

We sat and read scenes together, which I thought went extremely well. Again, another interminable waiting period with no response. And again, I was put off.

Sometime later, when it seemed perhaps the opportunity had passed me by, I was riding the subway, and who sits down beside me but Eddie Burns. That is not an urban myth. This happened. We both did a double take and, before departing the train, he said, "It looks like we're gonna call you." And they did. After one more appointment in which I read with him and a young woman then slated to play my character's love interest, I got the job.

The shooting of that film was a magical and special experience in a time when I had been sober for more than two years. This was, of course, the beginning of everything for me in New York as an actor, and I was working for free; everyone on the movie was working for free and it came to pass—long story short—that the film was shot, completed, submitted to and accepted by Sundance, which was then a budding film festival founded by Robert Redford. Admittedly, at the time I had no idea what Sundance was nor what it would mean to our film and the lives of everyone involved. All I knew was that it was a good thing. I traveled to Park City, Utah, to enjoy the second half of the festival and in the closing ceremony, *The Brothers McMullen* won the coveted Grand Jury Prize. Our near completely unknown, humble, heartfelt movie had there and then established a career for me.

Before this, it was a struggle to get noticed by agents, now they were contacting me with offers of representation. Casting directors were taking great interest too, and of course there was various other attention, including television interviews, print pieces, and parties. This was extremely pleasing and inspiring, though the most memorable aspect of all this, in retrospect, had nothing to do with any of those things. What stands out in my mind is the fact that just before I went out to Sundance—to enjoy what would essentially be the launch of my career as an actor—I started to drink again.

At the time, I was not aware of that being significant; people who abuse alcohol don't acknowledge the full truth of what they're doing and why. The habit, much of the time, is in service of the denial of what you're doing and why. And what I was doing was drinking again, suddenly, simultaneous to the beginning of, arguably, the most important time in my professional life.

So, I went to Sundance and had a marvelous time. I will say the drinking didn't necessarily interfere with that. With no dishonor to my forsaken sobriety, it probably helped it. It was an extraordinarily festive atmosphere, there were many parties, and it was a delightful time for a number of reasons. What was happening with me though, at a deeper level, was not delightful. I felt but was unable to acknowledge a profound anxiety. Somehow, just before I went to Sundance, I recognized what that represented: me entering into an acceptedly professional forum as an actor. You would think this would be a happy thing, and it was, but it was not only that. What I couldn't know or admit, because I didn't have the capacity to know or admit it, was that this also scared me. For all of my leonine pride in myself and my abilities and so much self-confidence that got me to that stage in my life, I didn't always feel adequate. I didn't necessarily feel ready for people to be constantly telling me how wonderful I was, and the drinking was in part my unconscious protection from seeing and feeling that.

After I'd picked up alcohol again, it accelerated quickly and continued at that pace for many months. It was daily and in great excess. I put on a good deal of weight. I remember showing up at my father's house at one point in this period and him commenting on that, and my deteriorating appearance. Oddly, I didn't resist this truth. I agreed with him and told him I saw it, too. He kindly broached the subject of my business being one in which appearance was very important, and again I agreed with him. He asked me what I felt about that. And I said quietly, "F--- it."

That's a good illustration of someone who's not loving themselves much at all. To know what you're doing is self-destructive, not only professionally but physically, but to continue in that direction shows not only a lack of self-value, but one to such a degree you feel it's only right to continue down a path of self-erasure.

By grace of the love it's been my good fortune to receive, my mother being a shining example of that, I've had an awareness of the importance of sobriety from early on in my life. As I shared earlier, I was sober right before I went to Sundance and that was largely in part because both my mother and father were sober when I was growing up. Our family has a strong genetic predisposition to abuse alcohol, but because of my parents' influence I got sober when I was eighteen—and then started drinking again in my early twenties right before Sundance, as I shared earlier. I hurt myself very deeply with alcohol until I realized I needed to get sober again. Though I resisted that impulse initially, which is common, I knew it was right. My mother wrote me a letter during this dark time, telling me how worried she was about me and how I was meant for something much better than what I was living. This, along with her enduring love, replanted a seed of sobriety that grew and then, sometime later, I was sober again.

I would go back to alcohol once more because although I had begun a more active conversation of self-love, I was still not ready to fully amplify it; I was not done interfering with my well-being. My use of alcohol was one of the most salient examples of how I would put obstacles in my path and be sure not to do the right thing to or for myself. When alcohol was in my life, one thing was certain: I would not have the opportunity to reach my full potential. And I believe that is the purpose of all our lives: to identify our gifts and fully express and share them, and to be happy. At various stages in my life, this time right after Sundance being the most apparent, I have actively damaged my own progress simply because I did not think I was worthy. And so, when my friend, Elizabeth asked me to express myself on the subject of success, this is the story that came to mind. As I expressed in the introduction to this piece, the greatest success I have experienced is self-love for the simple and profound reason that it is through this we are fully able to love others.

Peace with one's self is peace with others. Love of one's self is love of others. There is no ego involved in it. It is a proud and humble thing at once, as any and all mastery comes from being of service.

If you ever wonder whether or not you are making the right decision, taking the right action, and nurturing the healthiest thoughts and practices, ask yourself, *Is it guided by love?* If the answer is no, explore more until you are able to see what alternative decision, thought, or action, is guided by love and employ that.

And in that spirit, my wish for anyone reading this—what I wish for anyone in the world—is to know you are beautiful and gifted. You are here to reveal that beauty and those gifts as fully as possible and to love yourself and to share love with others. And with that, I wish you all the greatest success.

● ● ●

Next, meet Jennifer Vaughn, someone I've met through our shared love of books and networking. While Jennifer is the author of both award-winning and bestselling books, she's also a longtime television news anchor in New Hampshire. If there's one aspect of her dual career that has sustained her success, it's focus. During unpredictable and challenging times in her own life, Jennifer shares the challenges of focus and how she's made it a defining trait of her life.

Stories from the Heart

Jennifer Vaughn—Clear and Calm, the Practice of Finding Focus

Tens of thousands count on me to have it, maintain it, and never lose it, at least when I'm speaking to them. Focus, in my world, is the calm and clear presentation of facts, events, updates, and incidents as they relate to my state, nation, and world. It's the full-body experience of control and execution. My mannerisms, voice, approach, and presentation must meet my internal standards before they can be transmitted publicly. It's a process I've honed through my two-decades long television news career, and it serves me well, but it takes constant practice. When someone asks how I can possibly be entirely composed when I'm informing viewers about crimes so horrific they make my stomach churn, or breaking news so fast-paced it's almost impossible to keep up, my reply is always the same: a practiced focus from the inside out that keeps me calm and clear. Dependable. Steady. Is that as easy as it appears? Absolutely not! Focus wants to be elusive and fleeting, slippery rather than solid. Here's how I have learned to take away its shapeshifting powers to keep focus working for me, not against.

The parameters of my job are static. I work these hours. I anchor these newscasts. These are the knowns. It's the unknowns that can shake focus. When we're presented with a particular challenge or assignment in our work lives, focus can become scattered if it feels too overwhelming or isn't predetermined. Suddenly, we can't think straight, panic builds, and the project's expectations feel impossible. In television news, shorten the timeline to complete the task exponentially, and you can begin to understand the pressure of constant deadlines and no wiggle room for mistakes. Focus is how newscasts come together. Focus is the most powerful force in the room once we've wrangled it into submission. Recently, my focus has been challenged like never before, as I dealt with the long decline and then loss of my mother, and the ongoing and devastating health complications with my dad, often running concurrent to each other. At the height of the crisis with my mom, I would race from the hospital or a doctor's appointment to work, often without time in between, and gather myself enough to prepare for the newscasts.

Almost daily, I would receive calls at all hours, often right before I was on the air, or during. My heart would pound, knowing at any moment disastrous news might be delivered, and it would go first to my voicemail. I would scramble during commercial breaks to return calls in less than two minutes or scour the transcription of the voicemail for its purpose. It was jagged and frantic. I felt overwhelmed by guilt and sadness, was endlessly heartsick, and had never felt the physical ramifications of intense stress quite like this. My heart literally hurt, throbbing and spasming as I spent each hour of the day anticipating nothing but more trouble. Now, imagine experiencing all of that while you're live on TV. Somehow, I had to figure this out. I had to get my focus back.

To modernize this focus process so it could cover these horribly extreme months that have stretched out to years, I had to dial it in. I started by adjusting how focus began, first quieting down my brain by pushing out superfluous material so I could see the words in front of me. Ideally, I read through every story before it hits the air. I edit sentences that feel obscure. Whittle down excess words viewers don't need. I tighten and tweak. Familiarity supports focus, and giving myself an early preview of the newscast lends nicely into how my voice, body position, and delivery will adapt. I will strongly enunciate a particular word. I might pause mid-sentence for impact. When I have time for this prep, my focus is fully in my control and almost subliminal in how practiced it has become. Here's the catch: It isn't always that clear and calm, particularly when personal struggles arise, and I was loaded with them. The heavier lift is when I needed focus to be there, and even though I kept calling for it like I always do, it abandoned me. There are newscasts I cannot even remember doing during this time because I was so distracted by fear and worry for my family. When the phone rang beneath the anchor desk and I couldn't pick up the call, my body would tense, I'd start to sweat, and my focus was reduced to one clear and simple objective: Just ... keep ... breathing.

It takes work to get it back, and still there are moments when I feel I've lost focus forever. All that carefully cultivated calm viewers expect to see nightly is still challenged when the pattern of my day is interrupted or supplanted by more problems with my dad, kids, breaking news, or sometimes a high-profile assignment I am made aware of. Perhaps it's a live interview with a political candidate, state official, or expert in a fluid situation. Suddenly, a flurry of thoughts swirl, focus can't control them, and everything from my breathing to my heartbeat is elevated and anxious. It's shapeshifting again, and I am losing control. The very first thing I do is reach for a pen. The physical act of scribbling out notes or talking points on a notepad transfers the scramble of energy from my brain to my hand, and that becomes a tactile shift in the power dynamic. My body and mind are back in control.

Air is next because focus needs to breathe. When you're in a rushed state and your heart is shifting gears from cruise control to breakneck speed, air is crucial. I grab it. I force my chest to expand until it burns. Hold for several seconds. Release. By the second or third round, my heart is downshifting again, and I can more clearly express a thought. I am better prepared to deliver the information, or execute the interview, and give my viewers the clear and calm delivery they expect and deserve. My mind desires its comfort place; it knows it has a job and wants to do it well. Even though it will take hits with the inevitable stressors of my life, it does fall back in line with these exercises, and just like with muscle memory, my mind responds. Focus is very much like a body part. I respect it, but I will manipulate it when I must, and it has taken great practice during this difficult stretch.

Next, evaluation and adjustment. These are tools I use to expand my focus and make me better at my job and my life outside of it. It's a regular practice in TV to review and evolve. What could I have done better? In this audit mode I can find the holes in my performance—particularly in a high-stress, breaking-news scenario—and implant the preferred outcomes. With focus back in line, my brain can't tell the difference.

Beyond the crisis of the moment, this practice translates through all aspects of life. As a mom and author of seven books and counting, I have determined that our world often mimics breaking news. Maintaining a family, home, job, and dealing with illnesses, relationship dynamics, and the pressures of daily occurrences is heart-racing, emotionally charged work that engages every cell in our bodies. Evaluations and adjustments happen in real time, so our stressors become intermingled with irritants that push the boundaries of focused solutions. In the instances during which calm and clear become agitated and fuzzy, I deploy a different form of focus: one that listens rather than acts.

I learn more before I speak. I mull a thought before it can evolve into something unproductive. Focus, in this way—that careful practice of listening—shapes my understanding of who and what I need to be outside of the newsroom, for my family, and for myself.

When I lost my dad less than two years after my mom, focus led me through grief. Even through enduring sadness, focus keeps my memories framed around love rather than loss.

We are infinitely better positioned for success, and even peace, when we can apply focus as it serves us best. Working around its most loathsome traits, I have come to appreciate the almost indefinable qualities of what makes it so influential in our lives. Focus is achievable but be ready to work for it. I will forever remain a patient practitioner.

● ● ●

I'm so inspired by Michael and Jennifer. What did you learn from them? They both remind me of how focus can be such a driving factor of success.

In Exercises 5 and 6, we're going to focus on what causes you to lose focus, and get to the heart of creating situations and moments for you where what needs to be at the center of your attention is there for you on a consistent basis.

POINTS TO PONDER

Think. Write. Talk. Action. *(Because practice makes us our best.)*

EXERCISE 5: Staying Focused—Managing Distractions and Derailments

Name and describe 5 things that you allow to distract you.

1._____

2._____

3._____

4._____

5._____

Name and describe 5 things that you can do to work around each of these distractions.

1._____

2._____

3._____

4._____

5._____

Name and describe 5 things or habits that derail you and throw you off course.

1._____

2._____

3._____

4._____

5._____

In reviewing the above, name and describe the steps that you will take to stay on course.

1._____

2._____

3._____

4_____

5._____

Name and describe 5 absolutes. These are absolute boundaries that you place on yourself or keep so others don't violate your boundaries.

1._____

2._____

3._____

4._____

5._____

EXERCISE 6: You're the Star—Shine Bright

This is the Star of Awesomeness from the Constellation YOU in the Galaxy of Authenticity. The stars connected to you are your personal constellation and galaxy.

1. Consider the people closest to you now. They are the people that you interact with or who impact you the most. Place their names in the center stars (closest to you).

2. Consider the roles, habits, or activities that you have with each of these people. Place the description of those in the outer stars.

3. On the lines that connect the stars, write the A word that best describes the way you feel when you are with this person doing this activity. Or you may find that a D word (distraction, destructor, deductor, derailer, or drama) is more appropriate.

Here are several "A" words from which to choose:

Awesomeness	Allow	Acceptance
Awareness	Authenticity	Attention
Abundance	Align	Actualize
Action	Assess	Amplify

4. In this next constellation, be creative. Write the names of the people who bring you the most joy and consistently support you. Then, create your own stars and add activities that lift you up and create the A word feelings.

5. Next, create stars and activities for people and activities that you would like to have in your life.

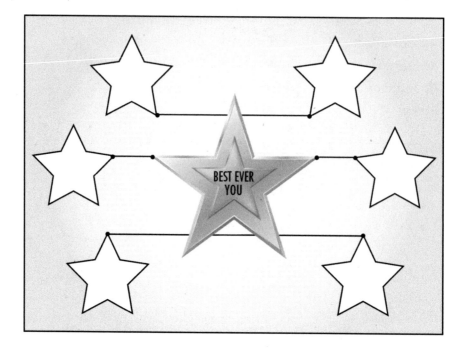

PART 2

ACTUALIZE YOUR SUCCESS

CHAPTER 4
PLAN

In the Fourth Factor of Success, we plan. We set our intentions in motion. We capture the momentum of our thoughts and become intentional in what we do. Motivation is a natural companion of intention and together they can pour focused, powerful energy into your creative engine. So, in this factor we get a move on it. We get clarity and we take action. Your life is powered by you!

In the heart of the Maine winter of 2021, ice storm after ice storm pounded the state before the snow started to accumulate, which was then topped off with more ice. As you can imagine, traveling even short distances was treacherous. Despite putting ice-gripping contraptions on our boots to walk our puppies and trying to be as safe as possible, we each, on separate occasions, took a nasty spill on the ice.

I landed on my left side, which completed my body-slamming ice adventures, as the previous year, I fell on my right side. My husband, ever the good Samaritan, was picking up the neighbor's garbage that the wind had spread in the street and yard when he took a nasty tumble and landed on his shoulder, which took months to heal.

For the first time in twenty years of weathering whatever Maine threw our way, we looked at each other and agreed: We were not doing this again next year.

SUCCESS TIP #24: Turn Your Dreams into Reality

And so, I went to Google to research and hatch our plan. We both knew just the place—South Carolina! We'd been there for baseball in March year after year now.

Google didn't let me down. I soon found the perfect place within our budget. "How does this sound?" I said to my husband, then read aloud the description: "Stunning golf-course views in your two-bedroom, two-bathroom condo."

"Perfect!" he answered.

I responded, "We're doing this. We are leaving Maine this coming winter from January 15 to March 15."

In unison, we said, "Let's book it!"

SUCCESS TIP #25: Map Out a Plan

And so, we did. While people back home were braving the cold and snow, I wrote most of this book from our condo on the golf course.

This didn't happen by accident, of course. It took planning. Once we decided to book it on January 15, we both focused on making the trip a reality. It was definitely a huge change and somewhat of a logistical stretch for us. Several things needed to line up right to make it work. Would we drive or fly? Would both dogs go with us? Would one of our sons and his dog go with us? At one point, we were worried we were going to be gone too long. One of our three cats is elderly, and we were worried about her, too.

We were grateful for our son Quinn, who was finishing up his master's degree in applied meteorology online from Mississippi State, for holding the fort down while we tried this life experiment. He watched the cats and his dog, Harley, and we did video calls with him to open the mail and pay the bills. Our oldest son, Connor, visited on the weekends to hang out, when he was not working.

SUCCESS TIP #26: Be the Hero of Your Own Story

My goal for you is to turn everything you confront into a success. From each experience you walk away with success and gifts, which are pearls of wisdom or learning. Have you ever had that feeling of *Wow, I actually did this!*? It's that moment where you are living your dream. You've done something you set out to do. In our case, we arrived in South Carolina and were ready to set up for the next six weeks. My husband and I were proud of ourselves for doing this. We had about two days of what I would call set up, that is, just getting acclimated to our surroundings, finding the grocery store we liked, and getting some semblance of a routine down. It wasn't a total break from reality. We both still had to work, but another bit of success is we were working from another location, which was another goal of ours.

We had a schedule of sorts or what we prefer to call a *framework*. This plan allowed us wiggle room to change our minds or pivot when circumstances changed. For instance, while the South Carolina winter feels like Maine's perfect summer, there is still inclement weather that might mean we can't do an outdoor activity we had planned.

We adjusted our plan as we found things we enjoyed doing together. One thing we love to do anywhere there is a beach is seashell hunt. It does bring out the competitive edge in me though. I'd elbow my way and trample over people like a Black Friday early morning to find a sand dollar, whelk, or conch shell.

SUCCESS TIP #27: Find Your Peace

People kept calling us "snowbirds" and we loved it!

I think you can turn planning on and off. You can restfully plan as well. More often than not, we need to rest in order to focus. To me in those South Carolina moments, my restful planning was being in the Myrtle Beach area and doing things we absolutely enjoyed. We were creating peaceful memories, and our energy was the most focused it had been in quite some time.

My husband, Peter, and I decided we would spend most of our time and energy on parks, hikes, walks, and beaches, and see what we could see. We also decided we would plan healthier food choices while we were there and take advantage of the ability to cook for two. We were able to cook healthier options, eat less, and exercise more. This created some calmer, more peaceful energy. That served us well. We didn't have any "disturbances in the force" and overall, it's been a great success!

You might laugh at this: I became a world-class shell collector while we were in Myrtle Beach. Honestly, I'm laughing as I don't even know what that means. I do know that from the moment we stepped onto our favorite beaches here, we found peace.

What mattered most to us wasn't collecting shells, but the peaceful feeling it created for us. Pawleys Island and Litchfield Beach have something the others don't have: the famous Pawleys Island shells. The first day I was on the beach I found one and I said to myself, *What is this?* I went to Google again and discovered that these shells are famous to these beaches and found only on the very north end of Pawleys and the southern end of Litchfield where the beaches don't quite meet due to an inlet.

If you find one of these shells, it is said that the island has blessed your presence, which is why Pawleys Island is known as the Blessed Isle.

Since the winter there felt like a Maine summer, we were out on the beach and there was hardly anyone on it. Some days had more than others and when you did see people, everyone was doing the same exact thing: Looking for sharks' teeth, shells, or just relaxing. Everyone talked to one another with eagerness in their voices to see what each has found or where they are from.

We both felt like the beach and the experience was a full-on reconnect to mindfulness and spirit. "Breathgiving" is what I renamed "breathtaking" to after being there. These connected experiences further grounded us in gratitude. My goal is for you to practice gratitude so much it becomes part of you as a person, like gratitude on autopilot.

When we realize we aren't entitled to time, we keep being reminded that every single moment of our life matters. When we realize that every single moment of our life matters, we realize that there's not much time for negative anything, and instead frame things with gratitude. This means that even in those darkest, desperate times, there is always something to be grateful for and to never lose sight of that light.

The real success there was in the moments and the focused, restful energy. We were thinking of our time in the sand, wind in our hair, the glittering ocean, gentle sound of the waves, and eyes on the sparkly beach prizes as the true measure of success. The restful energy flowed within our souls. We certainly feel blessed.

SUCCESS TIP #28: Explore!

With focus and intention at work and learning all we can about each beach, we also discovered this amazing peace on Sunset Beach in nearby North Carolina. It was hard to describe and then we found it: the Kindred Spirit Mailbox. You could feel yourself being pulled in its direction as you were walking. We didn't know about it until we found it and learned in reverse. We kept walking. We were probably over a mile down the beach past the pier when we saw it: a mailbox and a bench in the sand dunes.

We waited on the dune in a small line, while people were taking turns. Some were crying, laughing, quiet . . . all recording the moment and everyone peacefully allowing each other enough time in this moment.

My learning in reverse and more Google at my fingertips taught us that the Kindred Spirit Mailbox has grown to hold the wishes, thoughts, prayers, and dreams of those who walk there, essentially to share a secret to their soul or a wish, maybe even a dream.

SUCCESS TIP #29: Evaluate

Any new experience warrants an evaluation. I learned this long ago working in the corporate world and find it is useful in my life at times. In the corporate world, sometimes they are affectionally called "post mortems," especially if something went wrong that needs to be corrected.

I've found you can look at an experience afterward with these three questions:

1. What did you expect to happen?
2. What actually happened?
3. What would you do differently?

For us, we noticed we had removed expectations of anything while we were there. So much of our energy had gone into just getting there, that quite frankly neither of us really cared what happened once we got there. We felt like we had already won Olympic Gold just by arriving.

In looking back, what actually happened after about a week of settling in was that we learned we had much more clarity by removing and limiting distractions. We found it true that new places, faces, and environments stimulate and encourage creativity!

What we discovered we would do differently was two-fold. One answer was "not much." I loved this. In fact, we booked this same adventure for next year. The bigger discovery was that both of us wanted that level of peace and quiet in our everyday lives, while working back in Maine. But how? That was the real question. Was it the weather, the beach, the lack of winter? I think it was all that, but more. The answers were in how we acted and reacted during our time in South Carolina. When we removed ourselves from our everyday environment, we found clarity. We got to unwind from work and winter and warm up! South Carolina gave us a beautiful break to recharge to face the end of winter and "mud" season (springtime in Maine). We learned that we needed the battery recharges instead of going-going-going 24/7. It also gave us clarity to step away from any problem to see it in a new light. As I look back and write this, we have a new beautiful Maine garden in bloom, which has created even more peace for us.

SUCCESS TIP #30: Bloom Where You Are Planted

Bloom where you are planted is one of my favorite sayings. It's one of the ways I operate my life—happy and grateful where I am. This attitude also allows you to make the most of all situations that come your way. I'm very grateful to Barnes & Noble in Myrtle Beach for helping me live this saying. Not only did they say yes to having me in for a book signing, but they were incredibly supportive, and we had an amazing crowd and response. It was so much fun! I planned for one thing and got so much more from this event. I found a treasure in human form: Julie Beth Buckman. She appeared at my book signing and took such an interest in me and my book that I felt an instant connection to her. We were speaking the same language. It is my honor to stay connected with Julie and I look forward to seeing her this coming winter, as we've stayed connected, exchanged e-mails, and talked. Here she shares her story of how planning and several other success factors have changed her life.

Stories from the Heart

Julie Beth Buckman—Blooming Through Adversity

On this beautiful journey throughout my life thus far, I have felt much joy. I have also felt much pain. Through it all, I have believed, since I was a small child, that we each have a gift and passion to share with the world.

From the time I was very young, I hoped, dreamed, and planned on being a mom more than anything in this world. I married at the age of twenty-three and was blessed with my first daughter when I was twenty-four and my son when I was twenty-five. Life was very much like a fairy tale for me most of the time. However, I did have some obstacles to overcome. As time went on, I wanted a divorce. It was one of the most difficult decisions that I have and will ever make.

My divorce taught me some tough lessons and made me look deep within. Adversity is defined as a hardship or misfortune. I have always felt that I have the soul of a mermaid. I have no fear of depths but a greater fear of shallow living. This quest of mine to turn the adversity in my life from misfortune to fortune was found by seeking depth in my spirit and soul and enabled me to seek deep treasures. Exactly what a mermaid would do.

The journey within had begun. I spent my children's childhoods as a stay-at-home wife and mom, which is what I always dreamed I would be. As they grew up and explored dreams of their own, I kept having this feeling that I should start a yoga business. I had developed a deep love of yoga earlier when I was going through some very tough times. I often felt unbalanced within and at a loss of inner peace. I tried seeking it from other people, but that just left me more alone. That is when I remembered a line from my all-time favorite movie, *The Wizard of Oz*: "You have always had the power, my dear, you just had to learn it for yourself."

I decided in November 2019 to start Jewelz Yoga LLC to fulfill my dream to spread peace, love, and happiness to others. Through becoming certified in yoga, mindfulness, and meditation I learned some valuable gifts that I longed to share with others and have been blessed to do so. I learned how magical and calming one's breath is. It taught me how to create inner peace. I learned through reciting daily positive affirmations to gift myself with self-love, words of empowerment and kindness, as well as self-forgiveness when I wasn't at my best. This was a signal from within that I needed some relaxing, rejuvenating time to myself.

Adversity comes in many colors in life, and sometimes a move and fresh start are in order. My children and I moved to beautiful Myrtle Beach, South Carolina. Although we had vacationed there many times and loved it, we had no family or friends there yet. Still, it was just what I needed as the beautiful home that we bought right near the beach fills my soul with inner peace. To buy my own home and to empower myself to take responsibility and care for everything myself somehow felt exciting to me. It was like an awakening and a beautiful empowerment that is hard to put into words.

To this day, I begin every beautiful morning with a meditative walk along the beach. This allows me to collect my thoughts for the day and to let the vibrations of the ocean waves gift my soul with calm. Stopping along my meditative journey, I spend time refreshing my spirit with beach yoga.

This practice empowered me to once again look within myself. I graduated when I was twenty-two with an associate's degree in early childhood education, but I regretted not completing my bachelor's degree. Through the love, support, and encouragement of my children, I then embarked on the journey to complete my bachelor's in psychology, and within a year I graduated.

I have been deeply inspired and supported by my professors and have developed a deep love of positive psychology. Upon graduation I was accepted into graduate school. I am now well into completing my master's in marriage and family therapy. I have earned a 4.0 and do not see myself stopping until I earn my doctorate in psychology.

I feel most honored as I write this to have found out today that I have been nominated and accepted into the National Society of Leadership and Success. This is a very high honor, and I am deeply grateful and proud. This will nurture my journey to helping others by being part of a distinguished group of scholars who have earned a very high GPA to be a part of an inspirational network of world influencers.

As I meditatively walked the beach this morning to reflect upon my journey thus far, I found deep gratitude for all the challenges that I have overcome. I am most inspired to help others face their fears and overcome adversity in their lives so they can shine their light upon this beautiful world.

I have never in my life felt more empowered. I have been able to successfully grow my business, Jewelz Yoga, in my beautiful new hometown of Myrtle Beach. I teach weekly classes in baby and caregiver yoga, toddler Zen, mindfulness for children, as well as adult meditation and mindfulness. Also, I have been blessed to become a co-owner and editor-in-chief of *Jewelz Fashion and Lifestyle Magazine*, in which I write a monthly column "Jewelz Zen Zone," featuring articles on yoga and meditation.

As I always say, a mermaid's soul swims the deepest. I will love and embrace every beautiful moment and have learned to let go of what was. I meditatively watch the ocean waves and let go of the negative energy and embrace the good and positive energy. I pray to God every day that through journeying so deeply within, I am guided to embrace the treasures there and to shine my light upon our beautiful world. This is what life is about. As my mother always told me, "Bloom where you are planted."

● ● ●

Julie's favorite saying reminds me so much of when my husband and I first moved from California to Maine over twenty years ago. He had a new job, and it was very clear what he would be doing. I, however, was in this new place with four small children, re-learning and discovering everything. I kept saying to myself and our family, "Bloom where planted," and that is exactly what we have done here over the years.

Next, please meet Linda Pritchett. Linda is baseball family. Our son Cam stayed with Linda and her sons when he made that move to North Carolina. Since, Linda and I have become close, and I've learned a lot from her in many ways, including planning. Linda is an incredible planner by nature and uses this superpower to her benefit in multiple ways.

Stories from the Heart

Linda Pritchett—Plan Your Performance

Back in the 1980s, I worked for a bank, and I became what is known in the baseball world as a "utility player." I could wear any hat placed on my head. One moment I was a project manager in operations, and the next I was a product manager in marketing. Ultimately, it made me a jack-of-all-trades and helped me to be versatile in multiple topics.

While in the operational role, I had a boss who had a sign on his desk. It said, "Proper Planning Prevents Poor Performance." Each and every time someone stepped into his office, he had us read the sign out loud before we could speak with him about anything else. To this day, I will never forget that experience.

And as it turns out, he was correct. Proper planning truly does prevent poor performance. I think it was from him that I became a consummate planner.

Fast-forward to 2012. I had been married for fifteen years with two preteen sons. Everything was going great. I had been in the insurance business since 1998. In 2006, my best friend and I went into the magazine publishing business together. Since we are both great planners, we were able to conceive the idea in early June, come up with a name and logo, find a phenomenal designer, create a media kit, sell a bunch of ads, write a ton of content, and form a partnership with a national pharmacy for distribution. Away we went. Our first issue came out the first week in August, and we did this for many years. I was relatively happy in life. I did not marry until I was thirty-eight years old, and my single years were so much fun. I had two sons I adored and a husband who was a stay-at-home dad and a baseball umpire. He travelled a lot in the spring and summer, but he loved umpiring, and it made him happy, so it made me happy.

Then one fateful day in April 2012, I was driving my oldest to middle school when the phone rang. I thought I recognized the number, so I answered it. It was a very distressed man calling to tell me his wife and my husband had been having an affair for several years. Needless to say, my life was turned upside down that day. My husband came home from work early and told me he had multiple affairs over the course of marriage. To make a painful story short, I thought I could save the marriage if he was willing to go to counseling. He was not, so I knew divorce was the only option. It took us six months to get everything in order, to tell our families and our kids and to develop a workable plan to make it as easy on the boys as possible. And in the end, with a lot of bumps along the way, we made it all work out.

The biggest issue after the divorce became money, as we had debt and a tax bill to deal with. A few weeks after we separated, my youngest son asked me for lunch money. I went online to transfer money into his school lunch account and something told me to check my bank account at the same time. What I saw brought me to my knees. I had a negative balance: -$278 in my checking account and nothing in my savings. Because of the unpaid tax bill, the North Carolina Department of Revenue took the money out of my account. I was so mad, so embarrassed, so ashamed, so sad, so scared . . . the list goes on and on. And it was right then and there I decided to change my life. I needed a new plan. I was a woman on a mission. I packed my sons' lunches, got them to school, and started planning.

I made a decision that I would get out of debt in one year and would save $100,000 over the following four years so that at the end of five years, I would be debt free and have $100,000 in the bank. I started writing down all the things that would have to transpire in order for me to meet that goal. All I knew was that I would get myself in a position where I would never, ever have to worry about money again. I knew I had it in me and I also knew I was scared to death. So many changes in such a short period of time. But it had to be done and instead of letting the fear paralyze me, I let it fuel me.

I decided I had to go back into insurance; it was a field where I knew I could have unlimited earning potential. So, I sold my part of the magazine to my friend/business partner for $1 and went back to what I knew and loved: working in the senior citizen market. I brushed up on the products in record time, got myself out there, and started to do well.

I have always believed that when your intentions are clear and you write them down, the Universe will begin to conspire on your behalf and things will just start to fall into place. Little coincidences will appear, and serendipity will become a regular thing—but only when your intention is crystal, crystal clear. This is what happened to me.

An old friend introduced me to someone who was one of the most successful agents in the business. His area of expertise was one in which I wanted and needed to excel in order to meet my goal. He took a liking to me, understood my situation, and decided to mentor me. That was a game changer. I learned so much from him. My income soared that year and it continued to increase each and every year.

One day, I got a phone call from a local TV station. As it turns out, one of the producers read an article I had written in my magazine the year prior about adult children caring for their aging parents. She invited me on to the morning news program to talk about that subject. After the segment was over, she pulled me aside and said I was a natural on TV and they'd like to have me on again sometime. Of course, I agreed. Once every few months eventually became once a week, and I can't begin to explain how much that helped my business. My market is strictly pre- and post-retirees—sixty-two and older—and the most important thing to that generation is trust. Seeing me on television gave them a sense of trust I probably would not have been able to instill in such a short period of time on my own.

So many things like that started to happen to me. I was slowly able to pay off the credit card debt, and I am so proud to say that four years into my plan, I had $100,000 in my bank account. I literally cried when I saw it. I took a screenshot of it and that evening I shared it with my sons at dinner. I told them that through sheer perseverance and following a plan I had made years earlier, I was able to do this. I decided to use it as a teachable moment on how they can accomplish anything they put their minds to. At this point, they were fourteen and eighteen and could understand it better than when I first set out with my plan.

Of course, there were some bumps along the way. But it was because I put a plan in place and stuck to it, each and every day, combined with the serendipitous situations along the way, that I was able to accomplish what I did. And I remain grateful to this day for that desk sign that became embedded in my conscious mind: Proper Planning Prevents Poor Performance. It truly does.

● ● ●

These are both very touching stories, and I'm so proud of both Julie and Linda for being so brave and sharing them with us. We all learn from one another, and I know all of us could use more help with planning. When you plan for things, even if they don't turn out perfectly, you can more easily navigate a road map to your success.

Let's move on to Exercises 7 and 8. Here we will use my MAP

system—motivation, action, plan—to help guide you to form your plan. Then we'll journal our thoughts about intentions. As you are working through these exercises, don't worry if you get stuck and find yourself without answers! Don't get hung up on too many details and specifics at first. You can always make adjustments and you can also reach out to me for help. I'm always beside you each step of the way.

POINTS TO PONDER

Think. Write. Talk. Action. *(Because practice makes us our best.)*

EXERCISE 7: MAP System (Motivation, Action, Plan)

I use this exercise a lot in my coaching practice with clients. To do this exercise well, think about who, what, where, why, when, and how to MAP out your plan. With that in mind, answer the following questions.

Who: Who are you? What is your vocation?

_____

_____

What: What are your divine gifts that you will share with the world? _____

_____

_____

Where: Where do you want to make this magic happen? _____

_____

Why: What is your motivation? What is your why and how is it motivating you?

_____

_____

_____

_____

How: What action are you willing to take? Identify two very specific actions you are going to take to get there.

_____

_____

When: What is your plan? What is your time frame, and what steps are you going to take to accomplish this? _____

_____

_____

_____

_____

Date: _____

Signature: _____

EXERCISE 8: Journal Prompt—Getting Around to It

Here are "round-to-its." In each one, write something that you've intended to do, but have never done. Maybe you've said, "Not today, but I'll get around to it later." Elaborate your list of roadblocks for not getting these things done, and why or why nots in your journal or below. Do you see a pattern?

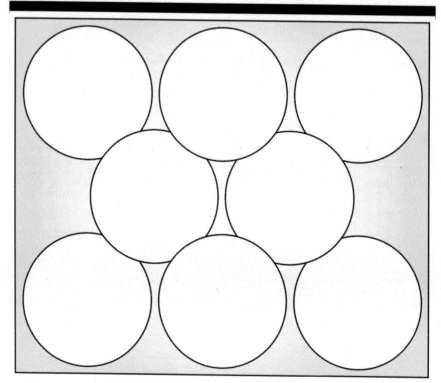

CHAPTER 5
ASK

In the Fifth Factor of Success, we ask. We reach beyond our circle and may even seek guidance from a higher power: the Universe or a deity. We may pray for a miracle. We learn from others and cooperate without fear or hesitation. We find grace.

Merril Hoge was drafted by the Pittsburgh Steelers in 1987. This fulfilled his childhood dream of playing in the NFL, and he used his saying, "Find a Way," to get there. He was with the Steelers until 1993. During his time there, he led the team in rushing and receiving in four of his first five years, setting a record in his third year for receptions by a running back. Along with Franco Harris, he is one of only two Steelers' players to rush for more than 100 yards in back-to-back playoff games. He was the Steelers' Iron Man of the Year two years in a row (1989 and 1990), and was named to the All-Madden team in 1989. In 1993, Merril went to the Chicago Bears as a free agent, where he played for one year until he was forced to retire early due to post-concussion syndrome. At the time of his retirement, Merril had the longest consecutive playing streak in the NFL.

On Valentine's Day 2003, Merril was diagnosed with non-Hodgkin's lymphoma. Through the difficult moments, Merril found inspiration through his daughter Kori, then nine, who, upon hearing the news, whispered, "Dad, find a way." On July 2, 2003, Merril was cancer-free. For all of his life accomplishments as an athlete and businessman, Merril's biggest impact can be felt within his family and community. A longtime board chairman of the Highmark Caring Foundation and Caring Place centers, which provide a place for grieving children, adolescents, and their families to cope with the loss of a parent or loved one, Merril's vision is to help all children know their value and importance, helping them to grow up healthy and whole. Each year, Pittsburgh Steelers wide receiver Hines Ward and Merril host the Hoge Ward Celebrity Golf Classic for Children to raise funds and awareness for the programs of the Highmark Caring Foundation. Merril says he loved playing in the NFL and loves working at ESPN but what he cherishes most is being a dad. He has used his "Find a Way" philosophy to become a better parent and to challenge his kids to take ownership for their lives.

I had the honor of interviewing football great Merril Hoge on The Best Ever You show back in 2022, and we spent about an hour together chatting about his life.

SUCCESS TIP #31: Ask the Universe, Find a Way, and Expect Miracles

Miracles are all around us—but we need to pay attention. Look for the extraordinary in everyday moments. Miracles are possible but some may be slipping by without you even noticing. When you do happen upon them, be grateful when life graces you in unexpected ways.

SUCCESS TIP #32: Throw a Hail Mary

A Hail Mary pass is typically made in desperation, a last-ditch effort to win. It carries with it an exceptionally small chance of achieving a completion, which is where the Catholic reference comes in. Hail Mary is the name of a prayer to the Blessed Mother for strength and help.

Do these passes ever work? Yes.

In 1975, Dallas Cowboys' quarterback Roger Staubach popularized the term "Hail Mary" to describe his miracle, game-winning touchdown pass to fellow Pro Football Hall of Famer Drew Pearson in a playoff game against the Minnesota Vikings.

In 1984, Boston College versus Miami (FL): Boston College quarterback Doug Flutie threw a 48-yard Hail Mary to Gerard Phelan for the 47–45 victory. The play is known as "Hail Flutie" and is generally credited with winning Flutie the Heisman Trophy later that season.

Who could forget 1994's "Miracle at Michigan"? No. 7 Colorado trailed No. 4 Michigan 26-21 with six seconds left to play. The Buffaloes were at their own 36-yard line when Kordell Stewart launched one of the most memorable Hail Mary passes of all time. The ball bounced off Michigan defensive backs Ty Law and Chuck Winters and into the arms of Michael Westbrook, giving Colorado a 27-26 victory and creating one of the top iconic plays in college football history.

As of February 16, 2023, Baker Mayfield currently holds the record after launching a stunning 70.5-yard Hail Mary against the Baltimore Ravens.

Hail Marys can also happen outside of football. You can throw a long ball in life, make that huge ask, defy the odds stacked against you, and get the job done. You can work a miracle. Trust in your abilities, ask your team to do the same, and give that ball a chance to hit its target.

By the way, the NFL has seen twenty-nine successful Hail Marys; three of them by Aaron Rodgers.

SUCCESS TIP #33: Find Your *Incredible Yes*

Successful Hail Marys are rare and, when they do work, are life changing. A more common occurrence is what I've termed for Best Ever You an "Incredible Yes." This is a moment where you said *yes* to something or someone and it changed your life. I love to help my clients anchor in the power of their incredible yes. Conversely, this can also be a moment where someone says yes to *you!* Ask other people what their incredible yes moments are, and you'll be sure to get a story. It's a powerful conversation and networking tool, a way to collect information from someone and share your own. "What is your incredible yes?" remains my favorite question to ask at events or when I meet a new group. I've had some amazing and inspiring responses over the years.

One of my favorites is from actor Michael McGlone, who describes his incredible yes this way:

After I gave my second audition for *The Brothers McMullen*, Eddie Burns asked if I would wait outside, which I did. He came out in a short while with the script for the movie in hand, laid it down and asked, "Are you ready for it?" I said yes. And indeed, this changed my life.

It was good fortune for Michael and good fortune for so many others who have come to love these actors and that film, one that was shot for $25,000, went on to win the Sundance Grand Jury Prize, and became, based on a budget-to-profit ratio, the most successful film of 1995.

What is your incredible yes? Do you have more than one?

_____

_____

_____

_____

SUCCESS TIP #34: Understand the Reroute/Redirect

Not everything is a *yes,* and in some cases a rejection is more common. If you've said no or heard no, buckle up, as you are getting re-routed, redirected, changed, possibly halted, and whatever else is ahead. In other words, what you wanted isn't happening. For whatever reasons, the Universe is placing a hold on what you are trying to do, and it can be frustrating and gut-wrenching. Even if you've followed every step in this book or others, and done everything you could possibly do, sometimes things just don't go as planned or as you'd hoped.

In these moments, we decide. Sometimes we accept the pause and other times we apply our foot to the gas pedal, take a different action, ask for something else, side-step naysayers, and find what we were meant to all along. Don't always allow a *no* to detract you from your dreams but understand the power of a pause.

We see that clearly in Cam's hand injury. He was doing everything he could to secure a future in baseball and make his grad year at Georgetown one to remember. He made the most of every opportunity, and still, Cam was rerouted. He learned how to focus and extract the positives, maintain his value and worth, and define the redirection. Often, things don't go according to plan, and you must go back to ask again or find new people to share in your process. It's not a straightforward path upward. Success is messy, like breadcrumbs.

SUCCESS TIP #35: Follow the Breadcrumbs and Cookie Crumbs

For me, it's all about cookies. I'm in constant search of others who leave great cookie crumb trails. In the classic fairy tale "Hansel and Gretel," the two children leave breadcrumbs (should have been cookie crumbs) on the path to get home. "Picking up the breadcrumbs" means someone ahead of you has left clues to their success if you are willing to follow the path. You can spot them if you are paying attention and observing. Listen with your open heart and mind and look for the breadcrumbs.

Information, opportunities, mentors, books, processes, wisdom, and more are left on breadcrumb trails. When you pick up the trail and the breadcrumbs you can learn more about success and apply it to your own life—and leave a trail for the next person. When you ask, "How did you do that?" or "How did you get to be where you are?" it's a clue to do more homework and find that breadcrumb trail. When someone asks you these questions, it's your cue to share and help the next person obtain the progress and success they seek.

Picking up breadcrumbs requires awareness and follow through. Pay close attention to both subtle details and larger clues. Be flexible and ready for opportunities. It helps to have a curious mindset to maneuver if you go down unexpected or unconventional paths. Both patience and tenacity are valuable traits since things must percolate. Fostering relationships and following referrals helps illuminate new paths, and doors open. When you pick up breadcrumbs, it means you are recognizing small opportunities or clues that may lead to bigger achievements or accomplishments. Each crumb represents a piece of information, a chance encounter, or a small win that, when accumulated and actively pursued, can ultimately lead to success. In all of this, it's important to understand that not every path is straight, just like life. In your best life toolbox, have tools ready to remedy setbacks, failure, and learning curves, while still maintaining your vision and focus on your goals and dreams. Embrace this concept and pick up breadcrumbs and cookie crumbs from others, and be open to lifelong learning that is so important to success.

SUCCESS TIP #36: Ask Big and Do Your Homework

You don't grow if you don't reach beyond yourself, your circle of people, and your experiences. Zero growth happens from your comfort zone. That's why we reach out and ask. When I asked Sophia A. Nelson to write the foreword for this book, it was a stretch goal for me. Sophia not only said yes, but it was also instantaneous. We'd been on each other's radio shows and knew each other well enough to have that instant collaborative excitement of supporting each other. I'm grateful I reached and I'm grateful Sophia responded. That's why we reach and ask. Here are more tips for getting comfortable with asking people for things you need or want.

We used to have this thing called cold-calling. Years ago, whether in person or on the phone, you asked for the sale or whatever outcome you desired. Cold calls are still happening today, but technology has changed how we connect. Technology seems to have mostly replaced this practice, as well as "no soliciting" signs, which we used to just ignore, but which are now posted just about everywhere. Today we may see a random and often automated DM hit our social media account or screen a call from a number we do not recognize. The point is, there can be thick padding in between our ask and the response.

If the request is real, it is often awkward all around. A *yes* depends on many things. Do you have the time? Is this something that will propel a career? Is this request feasible or attainable? To the person being asked, it often depends on the variables of that moment and perhaps even the value put into the request.

I believe it's important to know some facts about a person before you ask them for something. Do your homework first.

For example, when I asked Jack Canfield to help me with *The Change Guidebook*, I was respectful and genuine. I've been a fan of his for twenty years. I've had him on my shows. I have his book, *The Success Principles* pretty much memorized, and it's like five-hundred pages. I did my homework and formed a genuine connection. He's inundated with requests and asks of his time, energy, and expertise.

Because I did my homework, I saw how incredible his children's books with Miriam Laundry are. And, by the way, Miriam didn't just call up Jack randomly, either. Instead, she attended a retreat and got to know him. In 2012, on the flight home from the retreat taught by Jack, she wrote the first draft of her children's book, *I CAN Believe in Myself*. She set a goal to empower 100,000 children to believe in themselves. This goal scared her because she had no idea yet how to accomplish it, but she was determined. On May 7, 2014, she set the Guinness World Record for the largest online book discussion in a twenty-four-hour period! This meant that thousands of children from over twenty-nine countries around the world read a copy of *I CAN Believe in Myself* and left a comment on a blog about what they CAN do—all within twenty-four hours!

Miriam never planned on being an author. She had studied business in college. But she had discovered something she was extremely passionate about, poured her efforts into it, and through all of that, secured a lifelong friend in Jack. Her ask was supported by gratitude.

SUCCESS TIP #37: Be Genuine

Desperate people do desperate things. It's awful to be on the receiving end of that brand of desperation or seemingly improper use of a social media function. There is a difference in asking for what you want or need in a positive and confident way, where you *expect a yes*, versus being fearful and desperate and *hoping* for a yes while *expecting a no*.

When I was in my twenties, I oversaw marketing for wholesale clubs in the Minneapolis area. I was hungry and ambitious and had just graduated from college. I would have sold a membership to a newborn baby if I could. I look back and think, *How obnoxious!* It was that sort of energy that found success by kicking ass and taking names, but which was largely unsustainable. Our approach was one of nothing off limits, so we cold-called via telemarketing and walked into places with a pitch and a promise—anything it took to grow the membership base. Everything was personal, no cell phones, texts, or social media reach. We forced people to see us, and then talk with us, but for me, I almost stopped caring. I'd turned inward, away from the job to think mostly of my tangibles: income, bonus, raise, goals, buying a house, etc. I had dug myself out of debt from college and into a very nice apartment complex and was climbing the ladder. However, this job was a learning experience for me and not one I want to repeat. I saw myself behaving in a way that I now avoid. I can now easily spot other people behaving this way. Don't ever lose your authenticity—it will show.

SUCCESS TIP #38: Ask and Trade, or Pay What You Can Afford

If you wouldn't do something for free, why in the world would you expect or ask someone else to? It's an awful approach that leaves a prospective collaborator feeling burned. Now, there are some things that people do to be nice, and there is no charge attached, but make sure you're operating in the same manner. Give when you can, and never take advantage of someone's generosity of spirit.

Relationships can be very transactional in nature. This is neither good nor bad. It merely presents an opportunity for those who can't afford to pay for something they need to engage in a fair trade. If you are going to accept something from someone for free, offer value in return; otherwise, pay for the service. It preserves the relationship. The flip side to this is that eventually, you'll be in a spot where people begin asking of you.

SUCCESS TIP #39: Respond to Everything

When someone contacts you, respond in a timely period and professional way. Unless you're in mandatory response mode, you aren't technically obligated to respond to anything or anyone instantly. However, do it anyway. When someone has reached out to you, ensure they receive a proper, respectful response within a reasonable time frame, and personalize it. Do that not so much for them, but for you. Live and work in that grace. You may even design a signature response, such as a handwritten thank-you note or a phone call, to help people feel as though they have received something special from you.

SUCCESS TIP #40: Know Your Worth and Keep True to It

If I had received $100 every time over the past twenty years someone said, "Let's meet for coffee so I can pick your brain," I'd have a villa on the Mediterranean by now. People will generally take anything you are willing to give and often without offering anything in return. Make sure your worth and value remain whole when transacting with others.

I remind myself of this often, as people often expect free books, free editing, and so forth. I've been in their shoes with a startup business and magazine and worked tirelessly to build my brand. I think back to my very first Best Ever You crew, some fifteen years ago now (you know who you are!), who I couldn't remotely pay what they were worth even if I'd tried. Eventually, I did, and I went back and made sure people were whole. Pro tip: take care of everyone who has taken care of you.

Next, please meet Indiana Gregg and Del Duduit, sharing their stories of asking big and transforming their lives. Both also share a love of networking and know many people in their fields. Indiana Gregg is a visionary tech entrepreneur and the founder and CEO of Wedo, a groundbreaking social networking and fintech application. She leads an interesting life, and her superpowers are creativity, vision, and determination.

Stories from the Heart

Indiana Gregg—a Magical Three-Letter Word: *Ask*

As a budding female tech entrepreneur, the intoxicating allure of independence and self-reliance can be hard to resist. Like many before me, I was drawn into the narratives of self-made individuals, tales of daring people who, against all odds, built empires of success. This mirage of relentless independence seemed to shape the essence of what it meant to be a successful entrepreneur. Adhering to this ethos, I naively believed that asking for help was akin to admitting defeat, exposing a weak character. It took a challenging personal journey to understand that seeking assistance was not a sign of frailty but a testament to wisdom and the catalyst for exponential growth.

The initiation into my entrepreneurial journey was an exhilarating blend of sleepless nights, unfathomable challenges, and a seemingly endless reserve of determination. I was fully invested in launching my startup, embracing the thrill and terror that accompanied the birth of a new business. My worldview, framed by the notion that independence was the cornerstone of success, pushed me to take on every aspect of the business single-handedly. I naively equated asking for help with incompetence, an admission that I was not ready to bear the mantle of leadership.

But as the business grew, the illusion of the self-reliant entrepreneur began to crumble. The roles I had to juggle—product developer, marketer, finance manager, and team leader—became overwhelming. The long hours, incessant demands, and pressure began to erode my once unwavering resolve. The business I had nurtured with such passion was floundering. Still, I stubbornly held on to my belief, blinded by the misconception that admitting my struggles was tantamount to failure.

In the throes of this crisis, I attended a business summit, primarily to escape the challenges that were beginning to weigh heavily on me. One of the keynote speakers, an entrepreneur I deeply admired, offered an anecdote about his early entrepreneurial journey. He shared his initial struggles, the crippling loneliness, and the steep learning curve he experienced. Most strikingly, he emphasized that the most crucial moment in his career came when he acknowledged the power of seeking help.

His words hit me like a tidal wave. He argued convincingly that entrepreneurship is not a solitary journey. It requires collaboration, shared wisdom, and a humility that allows for learning from others. The idea was revolutionary to me. It dawned on me that I had been clinging to a detrimental ideology that had not only affected my mental health but also endangered the health of my business. He emphasized the power of a three-letter word that should be in every entrepreneur's toolbox: *ask*.

With newfound insight, I decided to embrace my vulnerability and ask for help. I reached out to a business mentor who had previously offered her guidance. At the time, the thought of asking her to help made me feel like a failure. However, given the words from the keynote speech at the conference, I phoned her up. She was extremely happy to be able to help and in fact told me she was hoping I would call her. She provided a wealth of experience and wisdom, helping me navigate challenges that had seemed insurmountable. I began to delegate more responsibilities to my competent team, trusting them and providing them with opportunities for growth. This reduced my load and allowed me to focus on strategic management and decision making.

In addition, I sought the assistance of an operations consultant. Her external perspective and expertise offered valuable insights into improving our business model, crafting effective strategies, and managing resources. The changes she proposed, although initially daunting, brought about a significant turnaround in my company's performance, and we were able to scale to over 14 million users as a result.

The transformation within my business was profound. The team, now more involved and invested, demonstrated a new level of enthusiasm and dedication. The mentor's guidance offered me the ability to navigate hurdles with confidence, and the consultant's advice significantly improved our operations and profitability. But the most dramatic change was within myself. I was no longer the struggling, isolated entrepreneur, but a leader who understood the power of asking for help.

My journey taught me that seeking help doesn't weaken leadership; it strengthens it. It opens the door to a wealth of knowledge and fresh perspectives that stimulate growth and innovation. It empowers teams, fosters a collaborative environment, and enhances productivity. More importantly, it nurtures resilience, providing the support needed to navigate the unpredictable and challenging world of entrepreneurship.

In hindsight, the decision to seek help was a pivotal point in my entrepreneurial journey. It taught me that vulnerability and strength are not mutually exclusive, but rather intimately connected. The bravest leaders are those who dare to admit they do not have all the answers, those who seek wisdom from others, and those who continually learn and grow.

Asking for help revolutionized my business, but more importantly, it transformed me as a leader. I learned that the burdens we carry become lighter when shared, that the challenges we face are easier to overcome when tackled collaboratively, and that the learning we gain from others is invaluable.

In retrospect, the misguided belief in the self-made entrepreneur is a myth that hinders more than it helps. Real success, I discovered, lies in the power of collective wisdom, in the relationships forged, in the humility of seeking assistance, and in the courage to expose one's vulnerability. The strength of a leader is not determined by how much they can carry alone, but by how much they can accomplish with the help of others.

In the end, my journey taught me that asking for help is not a sign of weakness but a display of strength. It reveals a leader who is secure enough to acknowledge their limitations and wise enough to appreciate the power of collaboration. It is a testament to the belief that we are stronger together than we are alone. And it is a powerful reminder that in the world of business, as in life, it's okay to ask for help when you need it.

Today, I stand as an entrepreneur who is no longer encumbered by the myth of the self-reliant leader. Instead, I am a leader who understands that seeking help is a strategic tool for success, a catalyst for growth, and a testament to wisdom and strength. The journey has not been easy, but the lessons I have learned are invaluable. I hope that my story can inspire others to shed the burden of unnecessary self-reliance and to embrace the transformative power of seeking help. Because in the end, it's not just about building a successful business; it's about growing as individuals, as leaders, and as a community.

Next, please meet Del Duduit, an award-winning author and sportswriter from southern Ohio. His work has been recognized by the Ohio Associated Press, and he has captured several awards for his books, including first place in the devotional category in the prestigious Selah Awards at the Blue Ridge Mountains Christian Writers Conference. Del covers the Cincinnati Bengals for the *Portsmouth Daily Times*, and broadcasts high school football games for WNXT radio. Here, he shares his never-give-up mindset with us and shows how it has served him well in his life and career.

Stories from the Heart

Del Duduit—The Power of Tenacity

Tenacity can be an extremely positive characteristic, but it can also be a negative trait if done with arrogance and without a specific goal in mind. Tenacity is determination, persistence, and not taking no for an answer.

Keep in mind, there are times when no definitely means no. This should be observed when it comes from parents, law enforcement, or your date for the evening. And it is especially meant for your good when no comes from God. If your parents tell you "No, you cannot skip school for the day," you should obey. You don't have to like their wishes, but you should always respect them. They know best—most of the time. If a police officer tells you "No, you cannot drive 100 mph," you should take heed or suffer and pay the consequences. Those consequences can be monetary or time.

But there are times when no might suggest "Don't give up."

Allow me to describe times when I displayed tenacity to accomplish my specific goal of getting to interview two celebrity athletes. I was in the midst of writing *Dugout Devotions: Inspirational Hits from MLBs Best* and wanted to interview New York Yankees slugger and All-Star rookie Aaron Judge. His reputation as a Christian was well-documented and I had plans to ask him a few questions about his faith to include in the book. The schedule I saw featured the Yankees coming to Ohio in Cleveland, and I reached out to the team's communication department to obtain ten minutes from Judge. I am a freelance sportswriter and have media credentials with access to the press box and clubhouses. I usually never requested permission but since the Yankees were coming to town, I thought it was best to reach out in advance. I knew the Bronx Bombers had a large media pool and I didn't want to get crushed by the sports writers in the clubhouse. My request was simple and to the point. I asked for a few moments with Mr. Judge before the game to discuss his faith.

Within a few hours of my e-mail seeking permission, I received notice that my request was denied. I was told no. Just like that. I could not interview Judge because he was in high demand and his time was precious. Although discouraged, I was not deterred.

The day of the game arrived, and I drove to Cleveland (four hours) anyway in hopes of getting to interview Mr. Judge. I did have a backup plan, but I knew that I would regret it if I did not try. The no did not carry any consequences. It was not an order. It was only a speed bump.

I made my way into the Yankees clubhouse three hours before the game. When I walked into the locker room area, I saw Judge sitting at a table on his phone. He was all alone. My target was 10 feet away. I walked up and said, "Mr. Judge do you have a few moments to talk to me about your faith?"

He said "Of course, I like to talk about that."

We chatted about five to six minutes and wrapped up. We had a meaningful conversation about how he uses his platform to inspire others and to tell everyone about his faith. A few moments later, a gentleman in a suit approached me and introduced himself to me. That was not out of the ordinary because staff tries to assist the media in various ways. His name stood out because he was the very same person who told me *no* in the e-mail. He congratulated me on interviewing Mr. Judge and told me he was "only doing my job to protect the players." All was good. I understood that and appreciated his honesty. He did not try to stop the interview because he knew Mr. Judge agreed to our conversation.

Had I accepted the original objection, I would not have been able to include Judge in my book.

Tenacity!

The other example deals more with follow-up and determination, which can also be described as *tenacity* or *having moxie*. One of the athletes I wanted to interview for *Dugout Devotions II: Inspirational Hits from MLBs Best, and First Down Devotions II: Inspirations from NFLs Best,* was Tim Tebow. But I knew that getting close to Tebow would be a monumental task. He is sought after and followed more than most athletes because of what he represents. He draws people because many have a desire to be inspired. People want hope. Most spectators who went to see him play baseball did not really want to see him make a catch in right field or smack a double off the wall.

In reality, the majority of people went to watch him play baseball or football because they wanted to see him pray with someone. Or they wanted to be encouraged by what he said. I was unsuccessful in my first attempt a year earlier to try to talk with Tebow but wanted another shot.

The former Florida Gator legend was on the roster for the Syracuse Mets and they were on the schedule to play the Columbus Clippers, just ninety minutes from my home.

This was my chance.

Minor League Baseball is not like Major League Baseball, the MLB. For example, one person can wear four or five hats. Such was the case with the man who oversaw the media. He also did broadcast and public relations, and about three other jobs. I contacted the Mets and obtained the contact information I needed. I sent an e-mail and left a voice message. A week went by without a response and so another set followed. Again, crickets. Nothing. No response.

Two weeks later I sent another e-mail and left a voice mail on his cell phone. Several days passed again without any acknowledgment. I was on my way home from covering a Cincinnati Reds game and decided to call the man again; this time it was about 9:30 PM. My thought process was that this person did not respond during the normal hours, so I gambled and went a different route.

This time he answered. We had a nice conversation and he apologized for not getting back to me. It was all okay. I acknowledged his busy schedule. During the chat, I revealed what I wanted to accomplish when Tebow came to Ohio. He told me upfront it was a long shot because of the rules established with the organization to protect the team from media onslaught. Most of the time, clubhouses are open to the media. But not this team. It was closed out of respect for the other players and for Tebow.

He told me he would approach Mr. Tebow with the request and get back with me. We went back and forth over the next few weeks prior to the game in Columbus. There were about twenty-five e-mails and twenty text messages exchanged without any progress or acceptance of my request. But I didn't give up.

Game day arrived, and I had no clue if I would be able to interview Tebow one-on-one. I went anyway. I showed up and the place was a circus. About three hours before the game, I noticed a young man in the press box preparing to broadcast for the Mets. I introduced myself and it was the person I had been corresponding with the past several weeks.

"I still don't have an answer for you," he told me.

I showed him pictures of me and my wife volunteering at the Tim Tebow Night to Shine Prom and some pictures of us with Tebow's mother, whom we met a couple of other times. He asked me to send them to him and I did. About thirty minutes later I was cleared and granted five minutes in the tunnel with Tebow.

Mission accomplished!

Had I given up after the first few calls went unreturned, I would never have interviewed Tim Tebow for my books. Determination and a "never give up" attitude fueled my desire. The hunt was almost as thrilling and rewarding as the conquest.

I have a similar story from when I was able to convince former Ohio State football coach Jim Tressel to write the foreword for my first book, *Buckeye Believer: 40 Days of Devotions for the Ohio State Faithful.* Mr. Tressel did not know me, but I reached out a few times and finally received a response from him. Once I was able to get the book in front of him, it was a good fit.

Obstacles are meant to be overcome. They are placed in your path to motivate you or bring discouragement to cause you to quit. I was taught in the professional sales world that a no is another opportunity to present your mission in another way. The key is to proceed with caution but with confidence.

Al Oliver, a former Pittsburgh Pirate great, World Series champion, MLB All-Star and Batting Champion, is a good friend of mine. He described me as "persistent without being pushy." You look for buy-in signs along the way. Keep going until the door is slammed in your face. There is a difference in the door being slammed on you, being closed, or left cracked open.

An attitude of humility and professional courtesy is another key. There is no room for arrogance or cockiness. If you believe in your mission, then stay the course and overcome obstacles.

I can do all things through Christ which strengtheneth me. (Philippians 4: 13)

This does not mean you can walk into a bank and rob it. If the cause is just and honest, then you have nothing to lose by having moxie and tenacity. Don't give up. Don't be pushy. Be resourceful and use your imagination. You won't be sorry you tried.

● ● ●

I'm so grateful that Indiana and Del shared their messages of tenacity and discovery. Great things can happen when you ask! Their stories are also continued reminders that anything is possible when you believe in yourself and ask of others.

As you proceed to Exercises 9 and 10, start to think about shared humanity as we move to reflect on who you are and who is around you.

POINTS TO PONDER

Think. Write. Talk. Action. *(Because practice makes us our best.)*

EXERCISE 9: Ask Big

Reach beyond anyone you already know and list five people you wish you knew.

_____

_____

_____

_____

_____

_____

What do you need each of the five people to do?

_____

_____

_____

_____

_____

What do you wish or want to happen as a result of asking big?

_____

_____

_____

_____

_____

Who is someone who has said yes to you before and helped you?

_____

_____

_____

_____

Pick one person from your list of five you wish you knew and contact them. Write any notes about them, your thought process, contact information, fears, wishes, and so forth here.

_____

_____

_____

_____

_____

_____

Be brave and bold. Go ahead and contact each person in your list. What was the process like?

_____

_____

_____

_____

_____

EXERCISE 10: Journal Prompt—Success Changes Things

In your journal, write about any fears you have surrounding success. If everything went your way or didn't go your way, how would your life change? Free write any goals, wishes, fears, and benefits about success. There is no right or wrong answer.

CHAPTER 6
NETWORK

In the Sixth Factor of Success, we network. We become active in the expansion of our dynamic community. We venture outside of established relationships to seek new and valuable connections. We expand our reach.

If I had to categorize the spectrum of networkers, it would go like this: A mediocre networker talks. A good networker listens. A superior networker learns. And a great networker connects. As I have encountered people, it seems they either love or hate networking and can't figure out whether it even works. They just don't see the value, perceiving it to be a roll of the dice. Perhaps someone is shy or introverted. Perhaps someone is crunched for time. Whatever the case may be, effective networking goes far beyond merely showing up to an event, handing out a business card, or trading contact information.

Ivan Misner is regularly hailed as the Father of Modern Networking. He has impacted generations and is a friend I have learned a great deal from. Ivan is the founder of Business Network International (BNI), which is a multimillion-dollar company with over 300,000 members in more than 11,000 chapters worldwide. Ivan is also available, generous, and professional. I can e-mail him anytime, if he's home or even working internationally, and he'll respond personally—even when it's not work related. It's one of the guiding factors of Ivan's allure, and why he's grown a network of trusted relationships that spans the globe.

Ivan adds, "While we are a multimillion-dollar company, we like to measure how much we make for our members. We are one of the few businesses in the world that measures and reports the success of our members rather than how much we made. For example, in the past twelve months, BNI has helped its members generate $21.7 billion in closed business for themselves. That number is higher than the GDP of more than 100 countries, according to UN estimates!"

Ivan has been sharing tidbits on BestEverYou.com from the very beginning, and I'm proud to feature his expertise on the website and in my own network. There's lots to be learned from Ivan on my platform, in his YouTube videos, on his blogs, in his books, and on social media. Beyond simply being an interactive figure, Ivan is funny, engaging, informative, and eager to tell you all about his wine cellar if you ask! Ivan is the author of a few of my favorite books like, *Who's in Your Room?* and *Networking Like a Pro.* Both books help readers turn contacts into connections and provide blueprints to build business through face-to-face networking. Further, Ivan's strategy to remove networking frustrations has enabled me and others to find like-minded, action-oriented people who support each other in ways that boost careers, experience, and confidence.

SUCCESS TIP #41: Think Like a Pro

Is there a secret to successful networking? If you ask Ivan, he'll explain there isn't simply one, but several. He'll point to a gathering of small things that work well together—like the perfect blend of coffee—that flavors the network with a comfortable, collaborative trust. If you ask him to drill down on that a bit more, Ivan will reveal four key changes you can make to enhance your own networking skills and create successful business connections that last a lifetime. Here are Ivan's Four Fundamentals of Networking:

1. Being selective (work with quality people)
2. Continuously add new people
3. Seek engagement
4. Share stories

Ivan breaks down how each works on his YouTube channels and in his books, but the takeaway impact is how the four fundamentals work together to take a smaller circle into a direct line of connections, add more members that meet your standards of depth and quality in relationships, make promises to each other to implement and support, and lastly, listen more. That can be a huge shift in how you've been approaching your networking opportunities, and something Ivan and I have spoken of often. At one point, I felt extreme frustration with in-person networking and confided that in Ivan. I told him simply, "No one is buying what I'm selling right now."

With his trademark brilliance, Ivan asked me a pointed question: "What was the room like?"

I responded that everyone was selling, and nobody was listening.

"Hear yourself back," he told me. "Next time be the listener in the room."

I thought about that, considered how it would work, and implemented it at the next event I attended. Now, when I mingle among groups of people, I listen and learn, ask questions, and try to become fluent in someone else's experience. Only when I'm the featured speaker at the front of the room do I focus on my own message or make the story about me. Otherwise, I'm the listener in the room, and I thank Ivan for showing me why that's so important in the art of networking. My husband and I have taken that message and shared it with our four sons, a practiced family trait we hope they will share with their own children some day.

SUCCESS TIP #42: Take Advantage of What's Available

Our youngest son, Quaid, calls networking a game changer in his academic growth. During his time at Rochester Institute of Technology he wanted to take full advantage of every opportunity he had. As a freshman, he joined the fraternity Phi Kappa Psi and learned how to make the most of every opportunity at the school. One of the biggest things his chapter pushed him to do was to go out and network with professors and alumni.

Quaid started to attend his professors' office hours regularly starting in the fall 2020 semester. COVID restrictions were in full swing, and all classes were remote and taught via Zoom. Quaid felt this new modality of instruction was limiting his potential to learn as much as possible. He saw the chance to supplement with in person and Zoom office hours as a path to bolster his understanding of each course and boost relationships with the professors. By spending these precious extra hours with course instructors, Quaid found renewed confidence and proficiency, and strengthened his knowledge of each subject. He pushed himself to find creative solutions to problems, and in an effort to assist me, he even brainstormed ideas for food allergy cures alongside his immunology professor.

Quaid also founded a club that served as a liaison between the College of Science and prospective undergraduate students. This helped him grow strong acquaintances with the Dean and numerous faculty members from many backgrounds, which then led to an invitation to share his input on how to shape the future of his college. Networking got results for Quaid and started the ball rolling for him to thrive in a challenging academic environment by reaching out beyond barriers to create a more satisfying and successful experience for him and others. The richness of networking also helped Quaid secure the Emerson Summer Undergraduate Research Fellowship, to work as a teacher's assistant for several classes including cell and molecular biology, and anatomy and physiology.

It grew from there. Once Quaid graduated *magna cum laude* from RIT in the spring of 2023, networking and his innovative work style earned him strong recommendations from several accomplished professors and a

Master of Science in the pharmacology program at Georgetown University. We are proud to have taken Ivan's lead and expanded it to reveal how networking can change lives, set trajectories, and become the building block of professional integrity throughout an entire career.

Let's continue to hone your networking skills—you can use them in all aspects of your life.

SUCCESS TIP #43: What Is Your Networking Purpose?

Picture this: you're in a room full of one hundred people and you have an hour to mix and mingle. Are you going to speak with everyone there? Are you heading to the corner to lean on the wall? Are you bellied up to the bar, looking for your next date? Next sale? Who in the room will buy your book on Amazon, and then tell a hundred of their friends to do the same? You get the idea; what exactly is your purpose in being there? What is your approach going to be? Begin with listening, but come up with a plan, identify your goals, and know who your audience is, to effectively network. Maybe even meet the one person who has the power or knowledge to help get you to the next level.

SUCCESS TIP #44: Put in the Effort to Be Effective and Valuable

Now, take that room above with all the people and their varied agendas and agree on one thing: each person has something to sell. Is the purpose for someone in that room to walk away from you or invest in what you're offering? Remember, for someone to leave the event aware of you is significant on its own . . . but for that person to follow up or even share your expertise in a referral is the grand goal. That's a lot to ask of others, so put yourself in their shoes: are you going to do the same for them?

Next, stay in that same room with the one hundred people and set a goal of getting to know one random person quite well. Don't worry whether that person walks away knowing all about you. Consider it a game: twenty questions to win a prize, with the prize being the chance to form a new relationship and eventually earn a referral or good word about your work and business. Your only job is to remember that person's full name and one or two key details you could tell another person. Being valuable to another is a gift you share, and one you hope to get back one day.

SUCCESS TIP #45: Create a Networking Bond

Twenty contributors have shared stories in this book, which reinforces the power of networking. When the foundation of this book began to take shape, I reached out to several extraordinary figures in my networking circle and requested each share a story as a contributor so that you can see the depth and value of networking at its finest. Like that perfect cup of coffee, your networking message must be the right blend of story, personality, humble prosperity, multifaceted experiences, and generosity of spirit to be effective. With that in mind, I reached out to those I considered successful through sheer perseverance. I tapped contacts, friends, and partners within my networking group who have risen above adversity to carve out happiness, fulfillment, and their own unique brand of success. To be here in the pages of my books, each contributor has something to offer, so I invite you to be like the listeners in the room—and hear about the factors of their lives that have the potential to change yours.

Maybe you'll feel inspired to contact each person in this book and grow *your* network, or perhaps discover something more powerful within your own life that could turn into a collaboration or new project. Consider this: if you reach out to even one person in this book, your world has expanded. That is exactly what networking is all about!

If you wonder how I built such a strong and varied network, I will tell you I learned to listen and invoke one constant: gratitude. This covers the experiences I've endured to become who I am, and what I feel for every single person who follows me, reads my blog and books, connects with me to ask a question, or requests an introduction to someone I value and respect. Along with gratitude, however, is another huge component of a successful network: intensive work. I will tell you blood, sweat, and tears have also built my foundation of success, and that is another constant you should expect once you decide to foster success in your own life. You must work—but quite frankly, that's where many people lose interest!

Like a student-athlete, medical student, entrepreneur, or anyone seeking life at a higher level, networking can be the catalyst at a critical moment of growth but only when the foundation is strong and secure. In other words, only after the hard work has begun can the fruits of labor be gathered.

I'm proud to share that I can riff about my network right from the top of my head. I know at least one important detail about each member, and once you're part of my world, you stay protected in my memory bank forever.

SUCCESS TIP #46: Make Everybody Somebody Important to You

I love this saying, "Be somebody who makes everybody feel like somebody." Etch a detail about someone else into your brain. Ask the one question no one else has thought of. Send someone away from your interaction with a smile. Pay attention and offer kindness for no other reason than you have the time and ability to do so. At any networking event, there will be disappointments and inadvertent gains. Plan for the former, but soak up the latter, because that's often where the heart of any connection can be found. There's no greater feeling than reconnecting with someone days, weeks, or months later, and having that person remember something about your meeting. Then, learn how to be the person who can do that for someone else.

SUCCESS TIP #47: Be Quick, Be Clear, Be Quiet

While you are making everyone else feel important, you don't want to be forgotten. Perhaps you'll be remembered for how you were so kind and your great listening skills. If you do speak, have something concise and memorable to say upon greeting another. This should be short and to the point, and perhaps have nothing to do whatsoever with your career and something more personal. For example, when I meet people, I don't say, "I'm Elizabeth and I'm an author and my books are this one, that one, and this one, and I'm in my mid-fifties and we moved to Maine over twenty years ago and we go to South Carolina in winter. Did I mention I love shells and oh, yes, I have four children and my husband's name is Peter."

Okay, are you asleep yet? Chances are the person just walked away or turned to someone nearby to escape or excused themselves to go do something else. Be quick. Be clear. Be quiet.

You'll usually hear my conversation go more like this: "Yes, thank you, hi, I'm Elizabeth Guarino and I make and donate chocolate chip cookies," or, "I'm Elizabeth and I write bestselling self-help books."

And then I ask a question of the person and stay quiet and listen. I may even ask to take out a notebook to take a few notes.

SUCCESS TIP #48: Go Above and Beyond

That segues perfectly into one of the most important points of being a successful networker. Whether you're the featured speaker at the event, a last-minute addition to the guest list, a nervous novice with no contacts, or a frequent flyer who knows every name there, set yourself apart by going above and beyond. Be memorable. No, that doesn't mean being obnoxiously self-serving, overly complimentary to a target subject, or imbibing heavily at the open bar. It means doing something unexpected, special, and personally relevant to your business, brand, and style. Here are my four networking *above and beyonds*:

1. **Call.** Give it a couple days and pick up the phone. Thank the recipient for his time or her advice. Make that person aware of why you valued your interaction.

2. **Write a handwritten thank-you note or letter.** There is significant power in old-fashioned missives. We don't do this often enough.

3. **Follow-up.** For a particularly memorable introduction or conversation, reach out again within twenty-four hours and then again *in one week*. People are busy, so be persistent if you have to.

4. **Pay it forward.** Follow that person on social media and comment, like, or share their messages. Make an introduction for someone else that could prove valuable to one or both.

Networking doesn't have to be the loathsome behemoth many believe it is. Once you can tame it, learn how to use it, and make it work for you, there is little that compares to the vast expanse of opportunities it can bring.

Let's take a moment to network with former Congressman Ric Keller and learn about networking. I've had the chance to meet Keller through our publisher, HCI. He is the proud author of *Chase the Bears: Little Things to Achieve Big Dreams* and a fantastic human. He's got a wonderful and memorable sense of humor and is one of those people that others are drawn to naturally with his charisma. When someone is likeable and approachable and helpful, like contributing a story for this book, it makes them a magical human being to encounter for they have your best interests at heart and trust you have theirs as well.

Stories from the Heart

Former Congressman Ric Keller—Guiding Principles for Great Networking

I'll tell you my favorite networking story. I was the speaker at a luncheon for the Central Florida Association for Women Lawyers. Afterward, one of the attorneys, Liz McCausland, told me about a big problem. Her mom had been locked up in a Vietnamese prison for over a year. Her so-called "crime"? Her mom had traveled from Orlando to Vietnam to attend a nephew's wedding and gave a radio interview calling for free democratic elections in Vietnam. There were no free speech rights in this Communist country, and it was considered a threat to the government.

Liz was on a mission to free her mom, whose name is Cuc Foshee. The challenge was Liz had tried everything—hiring lawyers, gaining press coverage, and pleading with the Vietnamese government—but nothing had worked. "Will you help me?" she asked. I promised to help. I even said: "We'll have your mom home by Thanksgiving" (which was three months away). I'm not sure why I said that, but my intuition told me to.

I didn't yet know how we'd do it, but when I got back to Washington, I learned that we had some political leverage. There was a trade bill pending in Congress that was worth over $10 billion to Vietnam called Permanent Normalized Trade Relations (PNTR) status. The key to securing her mom's freedom would be to block the vote on the bill until her mom was home safe.

I got the personal cell phone of Vietnam's ambassador, called him, and bluntly explained that Vietnam would not get a vote on PNTR status unless my constituent was set free. I explained that I would block the vote in the House, and Senator Mel Martinez, my colleague from Florida, would block the vote in the Senate.

Not too long after, a guard appeared at the jail cell door of Liz's mom. The guard said, "Cuc, you look sick." She said, "I'm not sick." He said, "Yes, we think you look sick. We're sending you home to America." The nightmare was over.

Senator Martinez and I met with Liz and her mom at an emotional homecoming party in Orlando. It was three days before Thanksgiving.

It has been seventeen years since Cuc Foshee was freed. Every November 12, the anniversary of the day of her release, I wake up to the sound of a "ding" on my cell phone. It's always a text from Liz that reads: "Thank you. This is the day you saved my mom's life."

What Liz doesn't fully appreciate is that *she* is the one who saved her mom's life. Her aggressive networking—reaching out to everyone she knew, connecting to those she didn't know, attending events so she could meet others beyond her network, and humbly and gratefully asking everyone for help—is what saved her mom.

Also, Liz is a generous and kind person who had been building authentic relationships her entire life. In her time of need, people were more than happy to help her or introduce her to people who could. For example, she knew some prominent attorneys who were friends with Senator Martinez and me and they helped by introducing her to us.

Important relationships don't just fall into your lap; you have to seek them out and make them happen. If Liz had sat at home, waiting for the right person to find out about her dilemma, or for the Vietnamese government to change its mind, or if she didn't already have a vast network of people she had helped through the years, the outcome may have been different. Since then, Liz and I maintained a close friendship for two decades. When I went through bumpy times, she was there for me more than anyone and provided wise counsel. It was a mutually beneficial relationship.

Liz is a great networker, and you can be, too. Here are three things to remember.

1: Play the long game.

Successful networking is all about developing authentic, long-term relationships with people you admire. If you network the right way, then you may be helpful to each other down the road. On the other hand, if there is nothing you can ever do to help each other, then you've spent time with people you wanted to hang out with anyway. I can't emphasize how important it is to play the long game. People don't want to feel used. Personally, I wouldn't ask any new connections for any meaningful favors for at least a year, unless it was an emergency.

We could all learn a lot from the late former Supreme Court Justice Sandra Day O'Connor about the value of playing the long game and maintaining relationships. Sandra "Sandy" Day went to law school with William "Bill" Rehnquist at Stanford. They sat next to each other, studied together, and dated. Bill even asked her to marry him. She declined the marriage proposal, but she treasured Rehnquist's friendship, and they remained close personal friends for thirty years.

Rehnquist was later appointed to the Supreme Court. After Ronald Reagan was elected President, he announced he would fulfill a campaign promise by appointing a woman to the Supreme Court. But who would he select as the first female Supreme Court justice in US history? Rehnquist recommended O'Connor to Reagan. It made the difference. Reagan selected the little-known Arizona state court appellate judge. Rehnquist and O'Connor would sit next to each other again—this time on the Supreme Court—for the next twenty-four years.

As a sidenote, I would eventually cross paths with both Justices after I got elected to Congress. I once introduced Justice O'Connor to a group of visiting high school students, and during my freshman term Rehnquist was kind enough to have breakfast with me and some other members of the Judiciary Committee.

2: Make it mutually beneficial.

Networking the right way is also about bringing value to the exchange. What can you do to help the other person? Perhaps the person you want to connect with is powerful, famous, or successful in their field. Don't assume that you have nothing to offer. You can contribute sweat equity, you can introduce them to others, or you can offer to help them in an area outside their expertise.

For example, shortly after graduating from law school, I met Jeb Bush while he was running for Governor of Florida. Traditionally, what politicians really need the most during a campaign is help raising money and getting endorsements. However, I didn't have any rich friends or political connections. Besides, Jeb was already well-connected and had the support of many affluent donors.

How could I possibly help? Well, I do have a sense of humor, and so I wrote a joke that helped Jeb deflect criticism in a lighthearted way. It became the opening line of his stump speech. The line was: "One of my opponents has accused me of running on my father's coattails. Well, to show that I'm running on my own merits, I've decided to go ahead and change my last name. I don't know what I'm going to change it to yet. But it's either going to be Reagan or Eisenhower."

Bush was eventually elected Governor and was helpful to me years later when I ran for Congress.

3: Introverts can be good networkers, too.

After I gave a talk on networking, a lady came up to me afterward, and said: "I'm an introvert. Sometimes I don't know what to say or do at cocktail parties." No worries. Here are two suggestions for introverts.

First, act like it's *your* party. If you were hosting a party at your home, what would you do? You would probably greet your guests when they arrived. You would introduce the guests to each other and point out things they have in common. Do those things.

Second, if you don't know what to say (or don't want to work hard trying to come up with clever conversation), then simply ask someone about their hobbies. "What do like to do for fun when you're not working?" People love talking about their passions. For example, I love riding motorcycles, standup comedy, and music. I could talk about them all day. Even if you don't share any of those interests, you can simply ask, "What's that like?"

The guiding principles for great networking are authenticity, reciprocity, and being in it for the long haul. It's a skill that you can be good it, regardless of whether you're naturally introverted or extroverted. Start by spending one hour less at your desk and one hour more cultivating authentic personal relationships. I wish you much success!

Entrepreneur Brian J. Esposito joins us with his life-changing story. Brian presently holds over 110 companies, 200-plus joint ventures, and proudly operates in 25-plus industries within his holding company, which is wholly owned by himself, Esposito Intellectual Enterprises (EIE). It's a unique model that he built for himself and protecting his world, assets, relationships, and reputation.

Stories from the Heart

Brian J. Esposito—Why I'd Take the Hit Again

High hurdles, speed bumps, heartache, and disappointments have plagued my path since I was a young boy. It befuddled and confused me. Why was I destined to face such dire and near constant challenges? Eventually, I became willing to chalk that up to being an entrepreneur in new and shifting industries and environments—and embraced the inherent risks of an aggressive approach to success. But, deep inside, I knew there was more to it.

In the most arduous moments, I felt an almost ethereal strength rising from within, protecting and guiding me. I lost my grandfather when I was just eight years old, and yet I always felt him close by. He was my first best friend, the one I desperately wanted to be with, make proud, and learn from. As I grew, I developed a craving to share space with older people to fill that hollowness in my heart left by my grandfather's passing. I sought to absorb their knowledge and wisdom to bolster my own fortitude to figure out the secret code to these pressure-filled circumstances I kept encountering and how to overcome them. Little did I know at the time, but the Universe and God were preparing me for the sentinel events of my life.

On a beautiful Sunday in February of 2016, my flight touched down in my favorite city, Nashville. After a quick stop at my home in Franklin, I drove straight to my offices in downtown Nashville, taking a lovely scenic route I had traveled a thousand times since moving there in 2014. About halfway into the ride, on the inner track of the four-lane highway, I noticed a pickup truck veering into my lane. At first, I assumed the driver was simply texting or distracted by the radio and would correct their course any moment. But within seconds, that vehicle was aimed directly at mine with another car to my right and nowhere for me to go. A crash felt imminent and unavoidable and yet, some force I cannot articulate removed my foot from the gas and spun my steering wheel rapidly to the left to avoid a direct hit. But we did hit. The sound must have mimicked an explosion as two vehicles traveling at a speed of at least fifty-miles-per-hour met each other violently and abruptly. And this is where it gets interesting.

In the ten minutes prior, a husband and wife traveling behind that pickup truck had called 911 to report an erratic driver. Further, they took the extraordinarily courageous step to block the lanes behind that truck to prevent other cars from passing too close to it. Because of this, when I cut the steering wheel sharply to the left and the truck slammed into me causing me to spin out across the opposite side of the highway, I ended up in a ditch on the side of the road. If that couple had not taken preemptive action to block traffic, I undoubtedly would have been in the direct path of other drivers, and this could have killed me—not to mention many others. As my airbags deployed and I tried to make sense of what had just occurred, I knew that I, and others, had just been saved.

Who does that? Who instinctively blocks traffic in the seconds before a potentially catastrophic event? I now believe that angels do. I remember the mysteriously ethereal couple helping me out of the car and then . . . I never saw, heard from, or was able to find them ever again. As for the careless driver? She was handcuffed and taken away on a stretcher. I later learned she was completely impaired by a noxious mix of drugs and alcohol. While I miraculously walked away from this accident, the real pain and biggest test of my life was still to come.

At that time, I had almost three dozen companies in my holdings, all based around my core business as a global beauty retailer, distributor, and e-commerce company servicing millions of customers around the world with over 1,200 brands. I worked alongside iconic celebrities, athletes, entertainers, actors, and actresses, building brands that began at a kitchen table and landed on the shelves of the biggest retailers in the world. I was thriving right up until the moment my brain decided it had had enough. I shut down, paralyzed into an obscure misfire that melted away all of what I'd just been. Simple calculations became complex and unsolvable, as my memory and emotional lucidity grew foggy and dim. Suddenly, every tool I'd sharpened to cultivate a formidable business presence was crumbling.

I became a sitting duck and everything I'd built quickly fell apart. By the following year, I'd lost everything, and yet the hits kept coming. The next year, near the site of the original crash, a famous singer drunk behind the wheel of a car slammed right into me. While this accident wasn't as bad as the first, I figured for sure God wanted me to find a new and darker rock bottom. I felt entirely alone. All those employees and executives I had generously paid and even co-signed for on homes and cars vanished, while brands I had helped launch and support declined to ship me any more products or include me on future projects. Many of them smugly ask, "Brian, what do you want us to do? We're not a bank." And, speaking of banks, I had those on my tail too, along with credit cards I'd held for almost two decades, who made millions off me, now turning me away with no life preserver. I couldn't find help or even a friend anywhere willing to lend a hand—when I had offered both of my own to them. I had to figure this out all by myself.

I was millions in debt, leveraging my assets to fuel my businesses, but I refused to file for bankruptcy. Determined to push through and rebuild from the ashes of everything that had already burned, I approached my resurrection with a focus on making myself whole again. I switched into a heightened mode of awareness that would make me stronger and smarter than I was before. With this new view I could finally see how I'd been surrounded by all the wrong people, and in that, I found only myself at fault. Instead of retreating into bitterness and anger, I chose forgiveness and a comeback. I dug into the dependable tangibles that always drove me forward: I loved people, and working with great ones who connected me to more outstanding talents who built connections and teams. I also had an uncanny knack of relating to everyone, no matter their class, culture, age, or profession. With those credentials still intact, I took an unflinchingly honest position to stitch back together my self-worth so I could re-enter the arena I had already conquered once before.

This time, I could sense negativity, toxicity, or trouble before I allowed any of it into my inner circle. I became the super-connector I had always been, linking people with opportunities while giving myself long-deserved credit for this previously underappreciated dexterity. I can now see how us connectors rarely understand our true worth and value because the monetary aspect runs secondary to what we seek to accomplish. As that revealed itself, it became the backbone of my new business: ensuring I was properly valued, recognized, and compensated for being the catalyst of connection, creativity, and production. Today, I remain proud and astonished at this new and improved perch over a hundred companies in my holdings, over two-hundred international joint ventures, a presence in over fifty major global cities, and operations in twenty-plus industries.

I am a better man than I was, so when I say I would take the hit(s) again, I truly mean it. My entire life model was wrong, and every event and hardship forced me to learn how to adjust midstream. I often reflect upon that Sunday afternoon near-death experience on the highway, and how it began the dissolution of the life I'd known. I am grateful for the trauma that followed, the evaluation of my choices laid bare, and the journey that brought me to this reflection. If I could leave you with one lesson, it would be this: understand that you do not need much in this world to be happy, that all of us can make something of ourselves, and success can be as simple as waking up each new day a little bit smarter, stronger, and wiser than you were before.

● ● ●

Again! More incredible stories of how networking is one of the most powerful tools for success that we can have in our Best Ever You Toolbox! In case you're wondering, today Brian is thriving, surrounded by some of the most amazing people, companies, projects, technology, solutions, and services. None of this would have happened if that accident had not occurred. He is extremely grateful for his life being ripped apart and ruined so it could be rebuilt better, stronger, and smarter than it was prior to that date. He knows if he could come back the way he did, that anyone can do it. It just takes time, resilience, dedication, and surrounding yourself with the right, ethical, and supportive people. Everything happens for a reason and it's up to us to analyze what that reason is, not to blame others for the situations we find ourselves in, and to do everything within our power to leave a positive mark on this gift of a life, and to always be kind and help people along the way.

What did you learn from these two stories? What's your current network like? Building connections with the right people at the right time could be mission critical to your success. Networking is a moment where we may ask or offer outside assistance to someone. We have a responsibility to each other and humanity as a whole to help others and do whatever we can, when we can. Remember that not everyone will ask for your networking help either, so it can be gracious of you to offer your help when you see a need or fit. Connections take us all to the next level.

Their stories make me think about moments in my own life where I have used the power of networking to help me and others. In particular, I think about this book and a few projects I've done with Brian J. Esposito. Because Brian and I know each other so well and we trust each other, we've done some amazing projects together and made some great introductions for each other along the way. Brian brought several people to me as possible contributors to this book, including Nando Cesarone and Indiana Gregg. Brian has opened his contacts to me many times for various purposes and I'm grateful. I also introduced Brian to the owners of the Old North State League where Cam played baseball the summer of 2022. As a result, they are now working together, and Brian was able to help the league make some immediate changes and improvements. Brian and I also co-authored a blog on BestEverYou.com that went viral called, "100 People to Watch in 2023." It was also a very popular blog on LinkedIn and continues to be seen. We decided we would work together once more to bring you this list of Networking No-No's.

Brian and Elizabeth's Networking Best Practices

Keep it short and succinct. If you're reaching out to a new contact, respect that person's time. Make your pitch meaningful and impactful. Don't force someone to scroll through lengthy e-mails or leave rambling voicemails. Explain in simple terms exactly what you're selling, asking for, or seeking to accomplish.

Be mindful of how you engage with introductions your new contact facilitates. Don't feel emboldened to start a new thread without including the person who is doing the work to introduce you to others. Offer to do the same in return.

Build relationships before requests. Nurture your new connections, whether that takes weeks, months, or years. Building trust takes time, and there are no shortcuts when you're asking for someone's business, expertise, or help.

Be tactful in how you contact a potential networking partner. Don't saturate that person's social media, e-mail, voicemail, or texts with the exact same message. Target the person's most historically responsive channel and allow some time for a response. Do not "reply all" to e-mails just to be seen by people.

Don't pretend to know someone. Being connected online or following someone on social media does not mean you are known to that person. Honestly represent every relationship. It's a small world, so be careful what you represent, given that your integrity and character are your most valuable resources.

SUCCESS TIP #49: Connect the Dots

The Best Ever You Network contains the word "network" intentionally, as I think this is a huge factor in our success. People in this chapter are dot-connectors; we connect with people who in turn connect us with others and while doing that, we're on the lookout for how it all works together and we include others.

Personally, I have moments where I drop everything I am doing to specifically meet new people and grow the network with focus and intention. I'm wired this way. It is something that comes naturally to me, and I love it when someone calls and asks if I can connect them with someone. The answer is *yes*. I consider dot-connecting one of my superpowers.

I was recently asked to speak about networking with my podcast at a huge podcasting event. I've used my podcast extensively to meet over six hundred new people in my life since 2010 when I started the show. Also, after each guest, I ask for referrals for new guests. I also use the Featuring You section of my blog in this way, as well as the magazine and conferences that I do. These are all ways to meet new people and grow the network and show that we all grow together. As a result of meeting Jack Canfield, for example, I was able to connect him with others who wanted to interview him for their important shows and events.

One of my favorite aspects of being an author with Health Communications, Inc. (HCI) is the network of authors they have. Whenever a new book is released, the author is on The Best Ever You Network, usually on the podcast in radio or TV format, in the magazine and on the blog. It's great to meet other authors and promote their books.

Let's move onto Exercises 11 and 12. In Exercise 11, you are going to write down twenty questions to help you be better prepared for networking. Asking another person questions is a powerful way to stop talking and shift the focus to someone else, while listening and valuing the other person to the best of your ability.

POINTS TO PONDER

Think. Write. Talk. Action. *(Because practice makes us our best.)*

EXERCISE 11: Twenty Powerful Questions

Write twenty questions that you can have at your fingertips to ask others when you first meet people in a networking situation or otherwise. Think of these as conversation sparkers and listening tune-ups for you.

1. _____
2. _____
3. _____
4. _____
5. _____
6. _____
7. _____
8. _____
9. _____
10. _____
11. _____
12. _____
13. _____
14. _____
15. _____
16. _____
17. _____
18. _____
19. _____
20. _____

EXERCISE 12: Journal Prompt—Begin with the End in Mind

In your journal, write freely about how you wish to be remembered.

_____

_____

_____

_____

_____

_____

What do you want people's perception of you to be?

_____

_____

_____

_____

What legacy do you want to leave the world?

_____

_____

_____

_____

_____

PART 3

AMPLIFY YOUR SUCCESS

CHAPTER 7
COLLABORATE

In the Seventh Factor of Success, we collaborate. We appreciate mutually beneficial connections and become strategic and generous in its power. Exposure generated through common interests generates limitless growth potential for all parties involved.

On November 1, 2022, my husband of over twenty-five years, Peter, received notice that he had been verified by Ticketmaster for Taylor Swift: The Eras Tour concert tickets. It was a total shock to me! On November 14, he was selected for ticket presale access codes to enter the sale the next day. He was able to log in and purchase six tickets for Section 314, Row 3, seats 17–22! I'm a huge Swiftie, and the surprise of this gesture filled my heart with gratitude. Thank you, Peter! Now, I realize there is a lot of controversy with how this process frustrated legions of Taylor Swift fans, so we decided to include as many people as we could. I reached out to a close circle of women, and we turned this into a life-changing event.

Once the tickets were secured, I immediately called my friend Jen and asked if she and her daughter Darby wanted to go with me. They were in!

With three tickets left, I texted our son's fiancée to see if she and her sister wanted to go. The remaining ticket went to our other son's girlfriend.

We started a group text. Jen got two hotel rooms and the girls shared outfit inspirations complete with pink boas, heart-shaped sunglasses, and frilly dresses. As a mother of four sons, this all-girl experience was new and adorable. I could picture myself again as a twenty-something, charging toward an experience that would become a memory each of us will carry for the remainder of our lives.

Loaded with handmade bracelets up our arms, two of us met Jen and Darby in New Hampshire and drove to Massachusetts. We met the other two, had some lunch, and then headed to the concert early only to be swept into lines of traffic hours before Taylor was set to hit the stage for opening night of her three-day stop at Gillette Stadium in Foxborough. Car after car loaded with screaming girls hanging from windows shared in our glee, as we exchanged bracelets and marveled at others' creations. *Aha!* So that's what the bracelets were for! I still have mine in a safe place even now.

The concert was an incredible experience, said to be a greatest hits tour that covers her now seventeen-year career. After seeing everything in person, from the production value, exhilarating comraderies in the crowd, and the raw talent of this woman, I'm quite frankly in awe of Taylor Swift and all involved in her tour. *Wow!* I wondered how she never forgot a word, remembered all the moves, and maintained that level of energy for what would be an entire year's worth of shows. I thought of the choreographers, the lighting crew, the wardrobe designers, the hotel bookers, the security team; a massive undertaking that is projected to net over a billion dollars in profits and boost the economy through public transportation and a spike in venue businesses. It struck me as the ultimate representation of a per-fectly executed collaboration seamlessly putting pieces together to produce a final product.

The fans collaborate on their own, in their own way. They share videos and social media posts, they enhance the experience to include all those who couldn't get to a live show, they create unified actions like bracelet sharing, or outfit collaborations, and they come together in joy and revelry. I've been watching videos from other cities complete with celebrities with bracelets up their arms, dancing and singing along with Taylor on stage. Even Travis Kelce, the tight end for the Kansas City Chiefs, danced and sang during one of her shows at Arrowhead Stadium, and wouldn't you know it, he seemed to know every word by heart.

Collaborations are inspiring and life-changing. Whether they're large, like Taylor Swift: The Eras Tour, or as small as a family meeting to discuss a future vacation, collaborations bring us together to experience something to which we all contribute our thoughts, emotions, and actions in order to elicit the best possible outcome. Collaborations make us stronger, and if you're not doing this enough, it's time to open yourself up to this vital component of lasting success.

SUCCESS TIP #50: Know That Life Is a Giant Collaboration

Everyone from each partner in a marriage to each member of a sports team, to the crew for a pop star like Taylor Swift, needs to be strong individually. But it's taking that uniqueness and talent and bringing it together in a collaboration that shapes next-level success. Without collaboration, we wouldn't have award-winning movies and gripping lyrics of songs that shape generations; we wouldn't see pictures that expose a new world or reach stars and planets in galaxies far away. Teams of people are involved in all things greater than self, and collaborations are bigger than any one person on the journey.

I spend much of my time and energy partnering and collaborating with people from all over the world. Whether it's a book I'm writing, a new issue of *Best Ever You Magazine* coming out, or a radio or TV show I'm hosting, I'm collaborating. Our family life is much the same way. Having been married for over twenty-five years and having four sons, our amazing collaborative life as a family is about helping each other be our very best. People often ask what the secret to a long-lasting marriage is and there is one word that always comes to mind: collaboration. I've had some wonderful partnerships and collaborations, some so-so ones, and some real doozies.

SUCCESS TIP #51: Collaborate Successfully

Awesome collaborators and partners often start with a leap of faith and a high level of trust. You don't know the result of the work ahead and can't force the future or rush the stage without risking harm to all and even the project itself. Things often need to percolate. Sometimes it can feel like you're stuck in a current; it will either deliver you safely back to the shore or push you deeper into the ocean. If things don't work out exactly as you first envisioned, step back and understand the lessons you are being taught. View the project with gratitude instead of attitude. You may need to step away if you can't handle the frustration of ambiguity.

Sharpen your project-management skills as they will suit you personally and professionally. Life is managing one thing after the next in both realms and chances are you'll trade-off between being the conductor and a member of the orchestra at various times in your life. Surround yourself with like-minded people and help everyone understand each role so the group stays on the same page.

I like to think the best of everyone I collaborate with, but generally things aren't always that perfect. It's critical you know what to do when you encounter a less than ideal circumstance.

SUCCESS TIP #52: Learn How to Navigate Collaborations

Unfortunately, collaborations can fluctuate and even become nasty. It would be nice if people entered collaborations with an attitude like, "Hey, if this doesn't work out, peace be with you and good luck." However, when we're building something greater than every individual involved, if and when things change, or people want to move upward and onward, or things start to turn, it can get messy. Sometimes collaborations start out great and then the wheels fall off. Consider a contract or collaboration agreement from the start to protect yourself, your ideas, and the integrity of the project.

SUCCESS TIP #53: Collaborate with Care

I'd say unprofessional or emotional behavior tops the list of fallout issues. Like an ongoing fight in a dissolving marriage, this may be and feel similar—wholly devastating. Often, the once cute sheep becomes a vicious wolf and leaves you wondering where that aggression, anger, and tornado of emotion are coming from, and when exactly it all went bad. Here are some warning signs that your collaboration is approaching a danger zone:

- Your collaborator is bad-mouthing you to others
- Trying to take all the credit
- Naysayers spreading negativity
- Shifting loyalties
- Threats
- Manipulation

You get the idea—just negative, cringe-worthy behavior that threatens your reputation, future work, and the joint project you're involved in.

One of the best ways to help prevent this situation from developing is crafting a collaboration agreement in the beginning. It can define things like goals, leadership, ownership, money, values, assumptions, behavior policies, and more. You'll know up front what the expectations are, and be protected with a baseline agreement in place in the event of the project failing or hitting an irreparable block.

SUCCESS TIP #54: Take the High Ground

I love the quote from Michelle Obama, "When they go low, we go high." It serves as a great reminder in situations to not be consumed by the negativity of a situation or person but rather see things in a different light. I've had brilliant and so-so ideas—and both kinds have been stolen. It still shocks me when this happens, and I promise myself every time to protect my next big idea from being pilfered. Learning the hard way not to trust a certain handful of people, I have also had to teach myself how to avert internal irritation from damaging my day, my work, my family. While I never intentionally engage with anyone who uses me, steals from me, or abuses my trust, if it does happen, I make sure I take away a lesson from the experience. Now, I take the high ground, disengage, tune out, move on, take care of myself, lick the wounds, and allow time to pass. If this has happened to you, I also suggest taking some space to examine your role in what transpired and take responsibility for your part. In one case, I trusted someone right from the get-go and didn't do anything to protect myself from the would-be idea thief ready to pounce on my good work. I took that collaboration at face value, failing to see behind the offer to proofread one of my books . . . until it revealed itself to be a plan to take my ideas and turn them around to pass off as theirs. I was hurt beyond measure but also angry to my core.

Conversely, I've finished projects with many collaborators, and we were effective, cordial, and entirely professional. Experience has proven that everyone needs to anticipate that what they start with is almost never what they end up with, especially if the project takes off, is popular, or gets accepted by a larger entity. That idea you first had may change and in order to make the project successful, you may need to adjust. One person may get picked up for something larger while a fellow partner isn't. Understand your role and who invited who to collaborate or partner up. Brush up on your strategic maneuvering skills—they are a key asset. I've developed eight collaboration non-negotiables and use them whenever I enter into projects with partners, friends, or new business acquaintances.

Here are my top eight collaboration non-negotiables:
1. Go all in!
2. Assemble a team of individual greatness that equates to total team awesomeness. Understand what you bring to the table.
3. Begin with the end in mind. Get everyone on the same page with the larger goal at hand. What is the final result you seek?
4. Create a clear process to the result you seek.
5. Tap into the momentum.
6. Understand how individuals within your group are motivated.
7. Give and get regular unfiltered feedback and measurements, while understanding things that won't or can't be measured.
8. Have an agreed-upon process, contract, or agreement in place for disagreements and project dissolutions. Have a process for

success and growth. Account for each best-case or worst-case scenario.

While I may have started out without a desire for formality, I learned that trust is bigger than most people. Not having a list of non-negotiables led to a lack of clarity, frustration, confusion, and bad partnerships. I've had to go back and apologize to myself and others for simply not understanding the full extent of what some people are capable of and for allowing myself to feel stunned by what they've tried to slip by me.

Collaborations are the backbone of success, and they work best when solutions are in place for when troubles arise. From bands breaking up to marriages crumbling, and partnerships staying together for decades, collaborations yield both great and dismal results; that's the nature of coming together with individual desires and expectations. That is exactly why common ground must be established to avoid disastrous conclusions. Give this fragile new relationship every chance you can to survive, thrive, and give back to everyone invested in it.

Next, please allow me to introduce you to one of our family friends, E. J. Yerzak. My husband, Peter, and I have known E. J. and his family for many years now. E. J. has written two amazing books in his Link Webber series called *Access Point* and *Denial of Service*, which won the 2023 Independent Press Award for Best Technothriller.

Stories from the Heart

E. J. Yerzak—Team Family

I'm an attorney, a cybersecurity expert, and an award-winning author. To the outside world, I have what you could call a successful career. Yet if you were to ask me to name the areas where I've been the most successful, none of the professional items would even crack the top five. Success, for me, is about family and a strong support structure of personal connections as the foundation for everything else. My résumé as a human being starts with being a husband and father.

I feel very fortunate to have met a wonderful woman I now call my wife and to be blessed with a young son who is the joy of my life. Being a husband and a father has taught me a lot about what success looks like and what it takes to achieve it. To be more specific, it's taught me that success requires collaboration. And collaboration begins at home.

As I was growing up, both of my parents worked multiple jobs to put me and my brother through school, to support us in our athletic pursuits, and to nurture our creative interests. At least one of them always seemed to be at my cross-country meets or my baseball or basketball games. I never quite knew how they managed to do it while working multiple jobs each. Truth be told, I never gave it much thought at that age. But it stuck with me.

Now that I am a husband and a dad to a young son, I have such an appreciation for parents who try to be at their child's events despite other obligations because I know it isn't easy. I work full-time as a cybersecurity consultant in the financial services space. Often, my job requires a lot of travel across the US and in some cases internationally to Europe and the Middle East. Wherever feasible, I try to schedule my work travel to avoid conflicts with other family and school events. And I am fully aware that the option of being able to do so would not even be on the table without collaboration at home, without a supportive wife.

My wife willingly put her career on hold to help raise our son. She is incredibly smart and compassionate and has a master's degree in social work. Social work is a highly needed but severely underpaid profession. The cost of daycare relative to the typical salary for someone with my wife's credentials and certifications made it an easy decision financially, even if it's not what she would have wanted professionally. In short, she would have worked forty hours a week just for that money to go right out the door to pay someone else to watch our son. Instead, my wife chose to reduce her hours to a per diem schedule so that she could be more involved with caring for our son. Eventually, she cut her hours entirely as my travel schedule for work picked up.

Many of my friends assume that I'm working all the time and I'm the one supporting my wife. While it's true that I am the sole breadwinner in our household at the moment, I know that support works both ways. Knowing that I am providing for our family enables her to be more involved in volunteering at my son's school and, as he gets older, managing an increasingly busy schedule of sports, after-school activities, and events. Knowing that she is on top of all of those logistics enables me to focus my work time on work. I am successful because of her, not in spite of her. I'm successful because we have found a way to complement each other's contributions to the household. It's that collaboration that enables success.

Collaboration at home involves many things, some obvious and some less so. First and foremost, collaboration is about trust. It's about knowing and believing that the other person has your back, and that you are both working toward a shared goal. In that sense, those collaboration skills translate very well into a professional workplace setting. If you can establish trust with your colleagues that you are willing to work together and not undermine the efforts of others, or put them down to make yourself look better, amazing things can happen.

Communication is essential to effective collaboration at home (and in the workplace). I think people tend to be in their heads a lot, having both sides of a conversation in our heads and planning things out before we ever get around to having the conversations out loud. But it's vital to have those conversations out loud so that assumptions aren't made that are wrong. I'll readily admit that I often assume the way I have analyzed a situation is the same way that anyone would analyze the situation, and this sometimes causes me to make assumptions that are left unspoken.

I'll give you an example of what happened recently in our household. I usually drop my son off at school in the morning and then go right to the gym before starting my workday. I enjoy those fifteen minutes with my son as part of our morning routine. On one particular day, my wife had volunteered to chaperone a school field trip. I assumed that meant my wife would be driving our son to school that day, even though she didn't need to be at the school until forty-five minutes after my son's drop-off time. I figured she would just read a book in the parking lot until she had to go into the building for the field trip. In my mind, it didn't make sense for both of us to make a separate trip to the school if she had to go there anyway. On the other hand, my wife assumed that I would still be taking our son to school as usual and then continuing on to the gym, consistent with my usual routine, rather than changing her morning routine. I even asked her several times what time she had to be at the school in order to chaperone the school trip.

What I neglected to ask her was whether that changed the drop-off person or time. With my son seated in my car and neither my wife nor I ready to bring him to school—each assuming the other was driving him that day—I realized the mistake. My wife and

I had both made assumptions and neither of us had communicated those assumptions. It was a learning moment. Despite a shared online calendar and confirming times for an event, something necessary for the collaboration wasn't shared in a way that was equally understood by both parties.

So, I come back to the importance of communication to enable effective collaboration. Communicate fully and communicate often. As I mentioned, my wife and I have a shared online calendar. We can each add events to it, from haircuts to sporting events to work travel. In our family, that shared calendar is essential to knowing where we will each be and who is covering what. But we also go a step further to inform the other person that we have added an event to a certain date, or to check each other's prior commitments before we add it.

Collaboration isn't just about the big things, either. Effective collaboration at home starts with the simple things, like calling your spouse or partner on the way home if you're stopping to grab a coffee or fast food to ask if they'd like something. It's grabbing your partner's favorite brand of something if you happen to see it at the store while shopping. It's offering to check an errand off your partner's to-do list if you realize that they're tied up in a meeting or at an event and won't be able to get it done that day.

Most of all, collaboration at home is about respect. Respect for each other's life goals, desires, hopes, and dreams. Life goals aren't just about financial goals. For our family, life goals include wanting to travel, exercise, spend time with family, and devote time to friends. My wife and I always try to do one family trip each year, but we also make it a point to carve out time for each other to take a trip on their own with friends. That involves planning around who will be staying home to bring our son to school and after-school activities for those particular days.

Collaboration doesn't come easily. It does require making a commitment to communicating effectively, whatever that means for you. It could include a shared calendar, as it does for us. Or it might involve sticky notes and other reminders left around the house. My wife will place certain things like store gift cards right next to my wallet and keys if she is worried I may forget to bring them to a store I am heading to—and she's right. I usually leave the house unaware that we even have gift cards to the store I'm going to!

Collaboration therefore requires a unique mix of communication, shared goals, and respect. It requires not assuming things but talking about things to make sure that you remain on the same page with your significant other. What works for one couple or set of parents is not necessarily going to be the same recipe for success for another couple or other parents. We've found a way that works for us. It has enabled me to be able to focus on my profession, because I have confidence that everything else is being handled. It's enabled me to be present as a dad, able to coach Little League and attend other sporting events and school performances, because I've been able to plan my time effectively. And it's allowed me to see the big picture, recognizing that my success is defined not by my professional accomplishments but by the type of person I am when I'm interacting with people.

I guess what I'm saying is that success requires teamwork. It requires working together and not trying to go it alone. Whether your support structure involves friends, colleagues, or, as in my case, a supportive spouse, finding those in your life to partner with toward a common goal can help you be successful.

Find yourself that person or group who will leave you reminders next to your car keys. Now, if I could only remember where I left my keys....

● ● ●

Boy, I can sure relate to everything E. J. just said! I love it when families work together! By the way, we can't ever find our keys either. With six of us coming and going in the house, it's been suggested we add technology to our phones that finds our keys for us, and we have a stream of endless requests for, "Can you move your car, so I can get out of the driveway?"

Speaking of turnarounds, it is my honor to have Lisa Gable join us in this chapter to talk about the importance of collaboration. She's a bestselling and award-winning author of the book, *Turnaround: How to Change Course When Things Are Going South,* and is recognized worldwide as a turnaround mastermind. As CEO of several organizations, and as a former presidential appointee, US Ambassador, UN Delegate, and advisor to Fortune 500 companies, Lisa has orchestrated and executed the successful turnarounds of well-known private and public organizations in all industries and sectors. She is highly regarded in business, political, and philanthropic circles for her ability to tackle difficult issues directly and with discipline and diplomacy.

Stories from the Heart

Lisa Gable—the Ripple Effect: Build Bridges and Enrich Lives

Motivated to connect and create opportunities, I embarked on an incredible journey of forming relationships with people from diverse backgrounds worldwide. This pursuit is a core part of who I am, passionate about making connections, eager to promote teamwork, and actively networking in all environments. During my travels and professional life, I discovered the value of partnerships with people different from me, which has broadened my perspectives. Working closely beside others who are thoughtful in our differences has enabled me to attain my own goals and achieve success.

Encourage the Art of Connection

Making someone feel comfortable and welcome is a beautiful art that only some naturally possess. It is easy to get caught up in our agendas and information silos and overlook the significance of genuine human connections. However, by being curious and embracing the uniqueness of each person we meet, we open ourselves up to incredible stories and valuable insights. From an early age, I embraced the opportunity to connect with others, recognizing how the new kid in school or the child alone on the playground was not a point of curiosity but a chance to learn and grow. When I turned twenty-five, I moved to Taiwan to study Chinese. With no friends in the region or knowledge of the language, I tapped into my childhood experiences on the playground and took them to a whole new level. I learned how studying a different language offered insights into the mindset of another culture. I was nervous but determined to put myself in front of new people and communicate with them. In that way, I overcame the language barrier.

I brought together fellow international students and organized a joint outing with Taiwanese students. We ensured European and American students didn't self-isolate with other English speakers so that everyone fully experienced life in a foreign country. I looked for chances to learn about each person's unique perspectives, gather recommendations for "must-see" attractions, and observe how they expressed their viewpoints. As we got to know each other, these conversations taught me how different cultures interpret and value information.

Create Opportunities for Engagement

How we treat people matters. The time and effort we put into someone's life can be the spark that changes their direction, helps them solve complex problems, and ultimately shapes our world. My long and prosperous friendship with Ana C. Rold, the CEO and founder of the Diplomatic Courier, is a perfect example of this. Networking can also be a lifeline during challenging times. When my husband, Jim, was diagnosed with a life-threatening disease, he was launching a technology start-up, and I owned a brand management company. Our adopted daughter was ten months old when Jim began a series of surgical procedures and treatments. I learned how to navigate personal difficulties while still pursuing a fulfilling career. I could only have done so with colleagues and mentors who ensured I had the opportunity to serve on boards and take on projects that gave me flexibility and allowed me to maintain a professional presence when I could not work full-time. Through this, I learned how meaningful relationships are. My husband and I have relied on our networks of support to overcome challenges, illustrating the power of collaboration in our personal and work lives. During that difficult time, I became even more determined to make the most of the nontraditional opportunities that came my way. I gathered a talented group to assist on projects and make work more efficient. I also took action to help others succeed because we all grow and achieve when we support each other.

Network and Mentor with Confidence

Mentorship has made a big difference in my life. Early in my career, I unearthed a knack for facilitating introductions and amplifying the voices of extraordinary individuals. Through connections and mentorship, I built a valuable network serving in the White House Office of Presidential Personnel, which oversaw the hiring and placement of thousands of political appointees. After looking at many résumés and conducting hundreds of interviews, I realized how important it is to help others find opportunities and connect with the right people. When you help others succeed, you can create a positive impact that extends to future generations. As the chair of a futuristic think tank called The World in 2050, I focus on mentoring individuals in their twenties, thirties, and forties. With intentionality, I seek out people from diverse backgrounds and ethnicities, as I firmly believe that the values of America transcend race and that our national melting pot is our greatest strength. I facilitate introductions among mentees and assist them in cultivating relationships, recognizing how they will one day make decisions that lead their communities in the year 2050.

Leave a Lasting Impact

My work has taken me across the country and globe, seeking to challenge my own opinions, find common ground, and advance opportunities for women. Collaboration within diversity is a force that transcends boundaries, enriches lives, and propels us forward. By actively seeking connections, embracing opinions, and fostering meaningful partnerships, we open ourselves to endless possibilities and lasting impacts. When we seize opportunities to develop teams enriched by experiences beyond our own, we proactively help others succeed, strengthen ourselves, and create a better future for all.

Make a Difference

You don't achieve success in isolation. All of us thrive through deep and meaningful relationships. Although the challenges you face may define life's moments in time, how you react to those challenges builds the leader you become. Move beyond transactional interactions as you consider your approach to working with others. Embrace a team approach that rises above temporary exchanges to cultivate enduring connections. Together, we can harness the power of collaboration and build a future brimming with potential.

● ● ●

What great reminders! I hope this chapter has recharged your networking soul! Let's keep moving to Exercises 13 and 14. Here, we explore in detail how to collaborate with others, and what to look for in others to help you along your journey.

POINTS TO PONDER

Think. Write. Talk. Action. *(Because practice makes us our best.)*

EXERCISE 13: Your Collaboration Style

Would you like to collaborate with someone? Who?

_____

_____

_____

_____

What would you like the outcome to be from a collaboration?

_____

_____

_____

_____

_____

List five fears you have about collaborating.

_____

_____

_____

_____

_____

List five benefits that will result from collaborating.

_____

_____

_____

_____

_____

What observations do you have regarding your style when interacting with others? What do you bring to the collaboration?

_____

_____

_____

_____

_____

_____

EXERCISE 14: Journal Prompt—Powerful Collaborations

Think of a powerful collaboration. It can be anything from a marriage to a famous rock band. Write about it here. Research it if you wish and add notes in your journal. Be sure to include what you like and dislike, changes you would have made, outcomes, and more.

_____

_____

_____

_____

_____

_____

_____

_____

_____

_____

CHAPTER 8
SUSTAIN

In the Eighth Factor of Success, we sustain. We comprehensively reinforce qualities that support world-class excellence in each area of our lives. We may need a great comeback, reinvention, or realignment to make it happen.

Sally Huss is over eighty years old. Over the last two decades, Sally has written more than a hundred children's books and a memoir. She is an example of sustained success, much like superstars that span years and generations. Think: the Beatles, the Rolling Stones, Elton John, Billy Joel—and Sally Moore Huss.

When her father asked her long ago in Bakersfield, California, if she wanted to be a tennis champion, Sally Moore replied, "Okay." She was ten years old and hardly knew what that meant, but it kicked off what would be a whole family effort to help Sally accomplish this lofty goal. It required hours of practice during the week and every weekend travel to Los Angeles for lessons. By the time Sally was fifteen, she was the number-one player in her division in the US. By eighteen, Sally was the number-one junior girls' player in the world. At nineteen, she was a Wimbledon semi-finalist. Sally came close, but never reached her goal to win it all.

Sally had an epiphany. Even if she were to win Wimbledon the next year, eventually someone would come along and beat her. Because she equated winning with happiness, she realized she could never be happy forever. That was a mindset shift that put Sally on a new path. She put competitive tennis away and embarked on a life based on happiness. She made the choice to be happy whatever the circumstances. That choice set Sally up for success beyond what she'd envisioned to that point, and it changed everything. In addition to tennis, when she was a young child, her mom noticed she was a beautiful artist and fostered this gift as well. As tennis ended for Sally, she eventually became a world-famous artist.

But first, Sally's talents brought her to television and film managing Paul Simon's music publishing company. She then married the man of her dreams, Marv Huss, who saw her tremendous potential, and with Sally, created a line of twenty-six Sally Huss Galleries across the country. Filled with Sally's bright and happy art, her writings, and licensed products, the galleries flourished. After the galleries closed in 2011, Sally did what she'd already done before: shifted, this time to write and illustrate children's books that give kids the tools and inspiration to overcome obstacles and hardships, while learning to value themselves and others. That collection now exceeds over one hundred books.

Sally's lasting lesson is an ode to happiness even when there's no championship trophy to take home. Happiness is a choice.

SUCCESS TIP #55: Secure Your Lifetime Achievements

I'm in awe of Sally Huss and have found such joy in working alongside her on ten of her books. I love her energy and enthusiasm and marvel at the depth of her creativity. Sustaining success is thorny and challenging, and yet Sally has mastered it like an art form, calmly taking the initiative in life to adjust, renew, and charge forward with happiness taking the lead. Her formula has earned Sally the inner peace we all desire and an eternal legacy of achievement.

The ER doctor down the street from us gave my husband a copy of *Younger Next Year for Men* by Chris Crowley and Henry S. Lodge, MD. I started reading it before him and soon learned there was a companion version called *Younger Next Year for Women*. The books in this series have remained *New York Times* bestsellers for years, so you may have heard of them. I buy and give these books out like candy to anyone who will accept them. The basic premise of the books is that you can "get old and live well" and these books show us how, not with concepts that send you down a strange path, but rather, through commonsense tips to combat the notion that we hit a peak early before a steady decline after age sixty. These books completely reject that idea, suggesting that you can have lifelong, comprehensive well-being with a few simple life adjustments, like exercising and eating right, and forming connections with others so as not to be alone as you age. Both books aim to give you lasting success well past your seventies and into your nineties.

SUCCESS TIP #56: Work in Reverse

What does your lifetime success look like? *Find Your Yellow Tux* by Jesse Cole starts with his eulogy. Jesse was moved by the question, "If you were to die today, would you be happy with the life you lived and the legacy you left?" In my first book *Percolate*, I ask readers to analyze the types of footprints they are leaving in every moment of their lives. I ask people in my coaching practice to work in reverse and write down how they would like to be remembered, the success each sustained to the end.

Working in reverse is powerful. It helps to align our lives. If I were to craft my own eulogy, it would reveal actions and accomplishments that I am most proud of. Something like this:

> Elizabeth Hamilton-Guarino helped people become their best, most successful selves. She inspired millions to understand the value of aligning their heart, truths, and energy, and bringing a sense of peace, grace, elegance, gratitude, benevolence, compassion, and collaboration to each person she encountered. A person who inspired millions to challenge

themselves to be their best, be unique, and live the life of their dreams. Elizabeth was a person who cared for others and would always give everything she had. Elizabeth was a devoted wife, mother, sister, and friend.

Go ahead and give this a try. Then, use it as a guiding framework to sustain success.

Coach John Wooden's book, *Pyramid of Success*, which I mentioned in the first part of this book, is filled with testimonials from many who say he's changed their lives. While impressive in quantity, it's in the quality of the lessons that I see the grandest value. Coach Wooden sets the boundaries of success, but each individual must achieve it in their own way and then sustain it. In each personal account is the happiness, like Sally's, that can be preserved and illuminated as we operate our lives with that as the foundation.

SUCCESS TIP #57: Create Comprehensive Success

Can success be illustrated? I've seen drawings and graphs of success that look like an upward line to the sky with no bumps along the way, like a smooth flight over the ocean in the worst storm ever. It's just not pragmatic or real. Success is so much more than a trajectory; it's a well of sacrifice, setbacks, and costs within a steady, sustained climb that can be relentlessly bumpy and nerve-wracking. Time also impacts the journey to success, periodically forcing a detour to rest, relax, recoup, and focus attention on other aspects of life. You may also feel stuck at one point or another and we need to account for that as well. That's when consistency becomes a practical point to reel us back onto the path. Think of consistency as connective tissue to success longevity.

In my coaching practice and on The Best Ever You Network, I help clients focus on six main areas of their life: Core, Art, Heart, Humanity, Spirit, and Sport. In these areas, I help people create a healthy balance or awareness when adjustments are needed.

THE SIX BEST EVER YOU PRINCIPLES

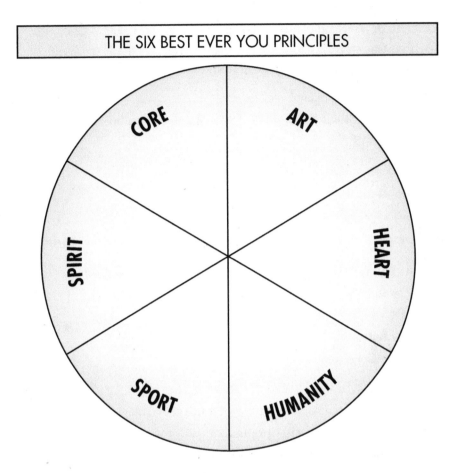

PRINCIPLE 1: The Core of You—Values

Focus Point: The essence of who you are—your values, beliefs, and behaviors.

Guiding Actions:

Live life with strong, unwavering values and character.

Ask yourself: *Is this in line with the essence of who I am?*

PRINCIPLE 2: The Art of You—Inspiration

Focus Point: Your unique, authentic self, as well as your talents and contributions to the world.

Guiding Actions:

Foster lifelong learning and utilize your skills and talents.

Ask yourself: *Does this celebrate my unique skills and gifts?*

PRINCIPLE 3: The Heart of You—Emotions

Focus Point: Your emotions, feelings, and awareness of self.

Guiding Actions:

Develop your best emotional intelligence.

Ask yourself: *Do I take responsibility for my emotions, actions, and behavior?*

PRINCIPLE 4: The Humanity of You—Compassion

Focus Point: Your role as a global citizen.

Guiding Actions:

Treat others with compassion.

Ask yourself: *How does this impact others around me and the world as a whole?*

PRINCIPLE 5: The Sport of You—Wellness

Focus Point: Your health and well-being.

Guiding Actions:

Champion lifelong well-being.

Ask yourself: *Does this moment or action contribute to my longevity and health?*

PRINCIPLE 6: The Spirit of You—Harmony

Focus Point: Cultivate harmony, inner peace, and contentment.

Guiding Actions:

Embrace harmony, inner peace, and being content.

Ask yourself: *Is my mind at peace and my spirit content?*

You can use this mini assessment as often as you wish. This is a tool I use with my clients initially; then throughout coaching we refer back to it often. In my personal life, I use this at least once a year to check in with myself to see where I am in the various areas of my life. You can give yourself a ranking of 1–10 in each section, with 10 being the highest level. This will help you figure out areas of your life where you need to become your best.

Is it possible to achieve a 10 in every area of your life? Who says you can't? I will tell you it's a strong *maybe*, but my most pragmatic answer is probably not all of the time for your entire life. Life ebbs and flows, and at moments, we can and do live at level 10 in many areas, but likely not all. And that may shift by the hour or day. I see this as more of an exercise than a guarantee, and my Best Ever You Toolbox helps us adjust during the times when challenge, setbacks, or unanticipated events interrupt the success we'd intended, hoped for, or are working toward.

SUCCESS TIP #58: Create a Foundation for Success

In all circumstances, consider where you started, where you are from, and what your foundation is like. If you know there is shaky ground beneath you, build a stronger foundation. To do that, let's begin with tossing out excuses and regrets. From here on, we set the rules for our own success and lay the planks for it to stand upon. Comprehensive success is a more realistic approach that examines every area of our lives to bring them back to an operational baseline that can promote and sustain success, while building a ladder to growth. Identify the beliefs and actions that hold you firmly connected to your success, and then visualize them happening in each realm.

In each area, what are your non-negotiables, beliefs, or actions to help you establish and maintain a foundation for success in each area of your life?

Core (Values):

Art (Inspiration):

Heart (Emotions):

Humanity (Compassion, Global Citizen):

Sport (Well-Being):

Spirit (Harmony and Peace):

SUCCESS TIP #59: Rack Up the Miles

Once you establish a foundation and start to best understand how to sustain success personally, it becomes easier to maneuver through life. With age, you develop a wise, experienced perspective that complements lasting success. Think of Sally Huss and how she reimagined her life as goals changed and happiness was challenged. Realize that dreams are a vital component of success, and becoming an expert in your own brand is not selfish, but self-fulfilling. Think of it as success grown from seed to harvest, having weathered storms and hardships, but enduring and strong.

Whenever our sons ask for advice, my husband and I remind them we aren't necessarily smarter than they are; we simply have more mileage. Success grown from seed translates into a likelihood of us having seen it, done it, learned from it, and lived to tell the story. It's always particularly impressive to meet people who have maintained one single expertise their entire lives, sustaining that success from a young age while navigating bumps and hurdles along the way. We are all experts in life. Share your lessons like we do with our sons. Teach tricks and help the young. Not all of us are granted the gift of racking up miles, so let's all share the signposts we've seen along the ride.

SUCCESS TIP #60: Build on the Momentum and Moments

Wouldn't it be great if we could reach the highest levels of success and then just stay there? Think of the superstar performer on a world tour; think of the energy and momentum demanded to sustain that success, night after night. Does that star tour every day of his life for years without rest? Of course not. Has she sustained success? Most likely, yes, however at some point, sales will eventually slow down and drop, and perhaps a new release fails to top the charts. That can create a recipe for frustration, burnout, exhaustion, and illness.

I've had moments in my life where I feel I have arrived at a success point and wish nothing would ever change. I also know I got there by deploying work habits, momentum, focus, and determination. In some cases, it took everything I had to get to that point, and I worried about how I could possibly stay there, when I felt empty and overworked.

Success can be in how you manage your projects and things that are happening in real time. And that's part of sustaining what we've already achieved.

SUCCESS TIP #61: Operate from Enoughness

Being a high-achieving type, I love this term: *enoughness*. How many trophies, awards, accolades, book sales, reviews, followers, likes, comments, and so forth are enough? Here are some of the questions I've been asking:

When is enough?

What is enough?

Don't let this get complicated. It's very important to recognize the rise, embrace the momentum, and then learn the warning signs of when to slow down. Success cannot last without this crucial balance. Don't think it's merely complacency and allow yourself to sink into an unsettled stall. Rather, ask those questions while you're already in cruise control. Am I satisfied? What area needs improvement? By micro-focusing on achievements and status, you can learn where the fractures in your foundation may be hiding.

Give yourself an assessment between 1 and 10 in each of the following areas, with 1 being the low mark (an area that needs improvement), and 10 being the high mark (meaning you got this!). Then, examine your results to learn how to better embrace the notion of enoughness.

1. Do you root your life in self-love and self-worth?
2. Can you allow yourself to feel success and accomplishments, or are you always seeking more?
3. Do you feel like there's unresolved business or work to be done in one or more areas?
4. Which ones and why?
5. Do you feel like you need improvement in one or more areas?
6. Which ones and why?

BEST EVER YOU SUCCESS ASSESSMENT

These evaluations can be a starting point or provide a moment of reevaluation. When I use these questions with my clients, I see many women who come to me for coaching giving themselves ones and twos across the board. They may be in a crumbling marriage or raising children while working so hard they feel as if they're failing everyone.

There is desperation within chaos, and that is when enoughness loses its effectiveness as a screening tool for success. There are blessings in marriage, family, and career, but goals and success can get swept away in the daily stress of juggling it all.

I remind my clients of their own power to shape their fate, to claim what they've earned, and to pause to reflect on a moment of success that can lead to fulfillment, happiness, and ultimately . . . enoughness. Think of a bad day as just that. One bad day does not equal a bad life.

I prefer operating from that place of appreciation and gratitude, allowing myself to feel my success and see what others do on my behalf, rather than scanning for constant chaos or shortcomings. In this, I find balance and a clear view of my goals and the areas of my life that may need some attention. Like Sally Huss, I can sit in enoughness, but still desire happiness in new and continued growth.

I've said for a long time and maybe in all my books now that you are the CEO of your life and every other C-suite title you can think of, from Chief Visionary Officer to Chief Compliance Officer and everything in between.

SUCCESS TIP #62: Set Goals Where You Are in Control

Don't give away your power; maintain your worth.

Sometimes, it is unavoidable and we are at the mercy of others. Who gets to play in the starting lineup on the team and who rides the bench? Who gets the job and who gets the rejection letter? These are the moments where we're at the mercy of others for our success. Their decision seems to seal our fate. Does it though?

Sometimes, we set the funkiest and loftiest goals and then realize it isn't 100 percent up to us to achieve the goal. We can get partially or mostly there, but may need someone else to help us along, and sometimes our fate rests in their yes or no.

Some people love goalsetting and others run from the practice. I'm somewhere in between. I've learned that I'm prone to setting goals that aren't in my control. For example, saying, "I'd like to be a *New York Times* bestselling author with a million copies of this book sold and thousands of reviews on Amazon within one year of this book's release." While it's a great goal, it's a lofty one that doesn't take into account very much that is within my actual control.

In fact, this goal is so out of my control that if I'm not careful it could leave me feeling unsuccessful, useless, depressed, and feeling never enough. Remember, you have limits to your control over what happens. You have actions you can do to help yourself along, for sure. There are some things in your power and things you can do to help meet this goal, but ultimately some goals give all or most of your power away if you allow them to.

I'd rather see you operate with enoughness and gratitude and have actions that support your goals and dreams. Much of your success in life is having great people around you, too, to act as your support system. You are not alone.

With this book, my success benchmarks are to reach you with my messages, to change lives, and other intangibles that can't be measured by conventional means. Would it be great to have my book become a *New York Times* bestseller? Of course it would be! My reality is that it is possible and that does remain a dream of mine, however, a series of smaller goals lead up to that possibility. I will always include that as a goal and work toward it, but I'll maintain a healthy, realistic perspective about it.

SUCCESS TIP #63: Create Healthy Boundaries and Best Practices

Burnout is real. Striving for success at the cost of your personal life and health is a mistake. Your health is paramount. Being in a cycle of any kind of health problem knocks people off their game. I've seen many clients in health crisis mode due to stress, unrelenting worry and anxiety, all dealing with issues ranging from chronic minor illnesses to major breakdowns. Now, there are times when you're legitimately stuck, or sick, or so burned out you need a long, sustained rest, but the key is to recognize the differences between demands and dangerous overwork. If you're caught in a cycle of burnout, problems and issues will set you back and put your future at risk. I know this on an intimate level. I've worked for overbearing bosses in my career, often working late, never pausing to consider my physical state or mental exhaustion. I've been that young mother with four children, working a job, traveling, managing life-threatening food allergies, and feeling like I was caught in a relentless tornado of demand.

To manage stress and worry, we must be cognizant of it first. I would toil to convince myself I was invaluable and then panic if I couldn't keep up. Finding a routine or balance felt impossible. But then, I made the best decision of my life and focused on being invaluable in the most important job of all: Mom. I moved away from the frantic pace of an office job and the travel it demanded, to work from home. It didn't happen overnight, but all that chaos and burnout that was harming me from the inside out, began to ease. I felt more focused and organized on my daily tasks, while knowing I was immediately available for my family—an enormous source of calm I had sacrificed to be an exceptional employee for someone else. Eventually, I designed a business that allowed me to remain in this at-home role and can now look back at this inflection point as a pivotal moment. I chose control over my own life, and it rewarded me with a brand-new level of success. This was my choice.

SUCCESS TIP #64: Life Happens—Be Open to Change

As I've just shown you, aspects of who you've been your entire life will always be with you, but be on guard for the unexpected. When we plan, God laughs, or so the saying goes, so keep in mind that change is inevitable. Our best futures lie within our ability to navigate change with grace. Success often depends on change, and one may take the lead at any moment.

Times change, things change, and we change. As you meet these next two contributors, think of how they took the concept of change and made it a flashpoint in their success.

Stories from the Heart

Tina Sloan—Sustaining Success and Joy

When the CBS daytime television show, *Guiding Light*, went off the air after seventy-two years on April 1, 2010, I faced the awful fact that my career as a soap opera actress was over. I was devastated, as I had been on that show for over twenty-six years. Though I had been in lots of movies and other shows, like *Law & Order SVU*, it was *Guiding Light* where I spent the days and years working. And I was in my sixties!

I wept for months. This was my family! The actors, hair and makeup crew, wardrobe, production staff, everyone was as close as we could be. Suddenly, we were all separated, and it felt lonesome.

So, after months of sadness, TV watching, and brownie eating, I felt a nudge to help myself and others who were lost like I was. I read somewhere that "the real sin is not dying but living an unused life." Unused life! There I was, giving in to the temptation to live an unused life by curling up on the sofa and watching movies and TV and eating brownies. How could I help all of us put one foot in front of the other?

In his final decade, Leonardo da Vinci said, "When you can no longer do what you want to do, want to do what you can do." I love this. Now, having just turned eighty, I can no longer ski, I can no longer run marathons—I ran eight in my forties—I can no longer climb peaks that I climbed in my forties—to 20,000 feet—but I can walk and hike. I love to put on my fitness tracker watch and see how many steps I can do. If I do 4,000 one day and 4,200 the next day, that is a win! It sustains me and makes me feel good about myself.

It is hard to stay in the game, but as Clint Eastwood said, "I get up in the morning and don't let the old guy in." He is in his nineties and that is a wonderful mantra to use each day. The "old guy" is the one who aches and would rather stay in bed and sleep all day. The "old gal" is the one I see in the mirror with wrinkles and think, *Why bother putting on pretty clothes or lipstick or earrings?* But by doing just those things, by getting up and by dressing with my earrings which have become my emblem, I am still involved in life.

After *Guiding Light* went off the air, I wrote a play called *Changing Shoes*, which I performed all over the country. I wrote a book, also called *Changing Shoes*, about going from sexy high heels to black flats. It's a book about aging gracefully and meant to help people like me, who were stuck. At the time, I was taking care of aging parents and worrying about my son who was a Marine in Iraq. I was at a loss in all this, so I invented a book to help people like me. And I made it funny by talking about aging on a soap opera. It kept me going through an entire decade. And I still go online and send it to those who I think may benefit from some of the ideas.

I remember some other things I did in my sixties for the first time which made me proud. Going to a movie, alone. The theater, alone. Out to lunch, alone. This felt incredibly hard at first but soon it was fun, and I felt so brave doing these things and not letting myself feel embarrassed. So much so that in my seventies, I thought, *What can I do to make myself feel relevant again?* So I decided to write a novel about a heroine in her forties. The book was called *Chasing Cleopatra*. The title character was physically strong, naturally beautiful, living a charmed life . . . and trained to kill, a heroine that was perfectly beautiful and could do everything physically that I could no longer do.

Sound like a soap opera? The book was successful, so I decided to write a sequel, *Chasing Othello*. Cleopatra was now a mother at forty-three for the first time. Quite a woman! I am now writing the third book where Cleopatra is skiing in St. Moritz with a devastatingly handsome Russian oligarch who is fighting Putin.

Something I do to give back are #Agingtips on Instagram. I do an amusing sixty-second talk, ranging from why we need hearing aids to being sure to hold on to the banister and to always take a flashlight. I am hopefully able to give my followers some insight into being older and still happy.

My husband of nearly forty-eight years is my greatest treasure, as is my son, his wife, and my three young grandchildren. I'm happy living a "used life" and grateful for our church and friends and work. I hope you all appreciate even small wins and the joys of family and friends.

Stories from the Heart

Liz Brunner—Sustaining Success in Your Next Chapter

Congratulations! You've done it. You visualized your dreams into reality. Maybe you've created a community or a business that continues to grow, but now what? Where do you go from here? You may even be asking yourself, *Is that all there is? Have I achieved "success" or is there more? And, what is "success"? How do I define it for myself?* I've certainly asked myself those questions in my four decades of being in the working world.

"Life is a journey, not a destination." We've all heard that phrase, and while I believe life is a journey, I also believe it's a series of "destination points," or success points, and each time we reinvent ourselves—or "recreate" ourselves, as I like to call it, we have the opportunity to find another level or definition of success. My own definition has certainly evolved as my non-traditional career path has unfolded.

Growing up, singing and performing were a big part of my life. I chose to go to college and study music at Lawrence University's Conservatory of Music in Appleton, Wisconsin. While there, in my junior year I competed as Miss Illinois 1979 in the nationally broadcast Miss America Scholarship Pageant. That experience not only paid for my education but offered me the experience to film a car commercial. Little did I know how much of an impact that one opportunity would have on me. Upon graduation, I became a high school music teacher and sang semi-professionally with a choral group that toured and performed in Europe. After a couple of years, I felt deep in my soul that there was something more I was supposed to do, although I had no idea what it was, nor what that next chapter would look like. I left my teaching position and quickly found a job in retail selling women's clothing, something I had been successful at as my part-time job during high school. (All that sales experience would eventually be a great skillset in a future chapter, although I didn't know it at the time.) While I attempted to figure out what I wanted to do next, I thought back to what it felt like to do that one car commercial, and the idea of a career in television was born.

With no other media experience other than that one commercial and the live Miss America broadcast, I bravely reached out to two television stations in the city I was living in at the time. One of them took a chance and created a position for me that had never existed before. I took advantage of every opportunity presented to me. This became my own graduate school. I learned how to be on camera, how to interview people with my little talk show, and I even did the weather! *Just because you've never done something, doesn't mean you can't. You just have to try.* That's the mantra I have lived by my entire life, and it's taken me to new, unexpected levels of success.

It led me to my next chapter, a twenty-eight-year amazing career in television at three different stations, culminating in Boston, Massachusetts, at WCVB-TV, the ABC affiliate—one of the top television stations in the country. At each TV station and with each role I held, I learned and grew. During my twenty years at WCVB, I reported on some of the most historic and remarkable events in recent history: 9/11, the election of the first Black president of the United States, the first double-hand transplant, and the Boston marathon bombings. I had the opportunity to interview many world leaders, including President Barack Obama and social icons like Oprah Winfrey. I was also fortunate that my hard work was recognized with Emmy Awards, an Edward R. Murrow Award, and Associated Press awards, to name a few.

Yes, many would call me successful. I was co-anchoring the number-one newscast in this market, but the industry was changing dramatically. The competitive climate and constant increase in expectations for all reporters made the work feel increasingly less magical and made me question my purpose in that space. Yet again, I felt a calling to recreate myself for a next chapter. *But how, in my mid-fifties, do I do that? What am I searching for and how do I find it? Is it more success? What does that even mean at this stage of my life?* I was certainly not ready to retire. So, after nearly three decades in the TV industry, I left. I launched my communications company in 2013 and never looked back.

However, running my own business was never, ever on my radar, and if anyone had said to me at any time prior to leaving television that I would be self-employed, I would have said, "Absolutely not!" I had no interest in doing that, and yet, here I am. If the only reason I could think of not to launch my business was fear, that was simply not a good enough reason to me. A quote by Eleanor Roosevelt gave me the courage to press on: "What would you attempt to do if you knew you would not fail?" What would any of us do if we knew we would not fail?

According to data from the Bureau of Labor Statistics, as reported by Fundera, approximately 20 percent of small businesses fail within the first year. By the end of the second year, 30 percent will not make it. By the end of the fifth year, about half will be gone entirely.

When the pandemic hit, I was cruising toward my sixth year with a full calendar of in-person clients and workshops and events lined up for the next six months. But as many companies experienced, almost every client and/or workshop I had on my calendar quickly dissolved. I was still in business, but rather than paying myself a salary, I felt the priority was to compensate the members of my team to help keep it all running. That did not serve me well when it came time to apply for PPP funding. My bank, a major bank, would not grant me any funds no matter how much documentation I gave them that proved I was in business. Eventually, I found a bank that offered me a small business loan. I'm still paying it back, but those funds gave me just enough to stay afloat. Thankfully, because of my diligent efforts, new and former clients sought me out for my media expertise in order to take their in-person presentations and meetings to the virtual world. A new chapter was born yet again.

I'm proud to share that in 2023, I celebrated ten years as the CEO and founder of Brunner Communications, working as a Certified Professional Communications Coach, executive coach, podcast host, and keynote speaker. Simply having survived being an entrepreneur (and through a pandemic), I consider myself to be successful. It took a lot of determination, perseverance, and a willingness to evolve.

"No knowledge is ever wasted." That is a quote from my grandmother, and it was repeated to me and my three younger brothers by our mother. There is so much truth in that quote. (Remember I told you about my experience in retail selling women's clothing? An important skillset learned because when you are self-employed, you are always selling yourself and/or your services.) Every experience—good and bad—is knowledge and when you connect the dots of those experiences, themes and patterns emerge. They can lead you to create next chapters, to recreate your life. I call it "recreation" because all that knowledge and experience is carried forward to create the next chapter.

Recreating a successful next chapter, a new life, and sustaining it does *not* happen by accident. It's one thing to have a vision, it's another to implement it. It takes doing the hard work, including the inner personal-development work. It takes a commitment to embrace continuous growth and consistent habits, and a spirit of determination, perseverance, and preparation. But let's be real. Life can get in the way. Responsibilities can get in the way. You may lose your passion or even lose your "mojo" and wonder why you're doing what you're doing in the first place. That is simply part of being human. In the first years of growing my business, I loved the work, but I was traveling across the country every week to work with clients. Self-care, exercise, and time to simply think and be creative often went by the wayside. I had to figure out how to get off—or at least slow down—the travel treadmill I was on and get back to the positive habits that made me feel mentally, emotionally, and physically strong. I also had to find some compassion for myself.

Sustaining success in that next chapter is also about *evolving*. Evolving through the tough times, handling the curveballs that life will throw at you. It takes resilience and developing an inner strength to meet those challenges head-on. Some of those experiences may even feel like failures, but failure is only a failure if you don't learn the lesson. For me, there are so many lessons learned: always pay yourself a salary, even if it's a small amount; how to be a boss and work with members of your team so they each feel valued and appreciated; how to evolve and grow a business even without an MBA, to name a few.

Perhaps one of the most challenging aspects of sustaining success may be getting out of your own way. If you are a Type A personality (and there is nothing wrong with that, I'm one of those, too), you may feel you have to continue to strive and drive and set higher goals. I'm all for goals, but it's important to acknowledge what you have achieved. You may or may not receive validation from the outside world, but *you* know what you've done. Find value in who you are, and own all of it, the highs and the lows. Pause, and take some time to appreciate and celebrate all that you have accomplished no matter how big or small. When I made it to year five of my business, I celebrated by buying myself a beautiful red Prada handbag. I'm not into designer labels and had never bought a designer bag before, but it felt good to treat myself, to recognize all my effort. When we pause to appreciate our own personal success, we are building a strong foundation for future growth and success.

Sustaining success in every chapter of our lives also requires passion and purpose. They are inextricably linked. With each of my career chapters, I've spent time pondering these questions: what do passion and purpose mean to me? I believe passion is about what brings you joy; it's what you love to do, what your interests are, and perhaps what you want to learn more about. Being passionate gives you a reason to get out of bed every morning.

Your purpose is the reason *why* you do what you do. It gives your life direction because it revolves around your unique gifts and talents and using them to make a positive impact in the world. Questioning one's purpose is one of the most uniquely beautiful and equally frustrating parts about the human experience. It's one of the reasons I love doing my podcast, "Live Your Best Life with Liz Brunner." The stories my guests share about creating their next chapters, their resilience, and sustaining a new level of success, are filled with passion and purpose.

Having a passion and purpose gives me a clear vision of how I want to live in this chapter and future chapters of my life, both personally and professionally. That vision is to teach, motivate, and inspire people to live their best life, whatever that means for them. Using the gifts and talents I believe I have been blessed with to help others achieve their own goals gives my life meaning and purpose today. I often see my clients' growth before they do, but when they see it, when they *feel* it, it's the best feeling in the world to me. If I can continue to do that, that is sustaining success in the most authentic way possible.

In many ways, I've come full circle. I've always been a teacher and a storyteller. I was teaching music to my high school students and singing stories with the adult semi-professional touring choral group. While on television, I shared other people's stories. As a coach, I'm teaching others how to tell their stories. And now, having written my first book, *Dare to Own You: Taking Your Authenticity and Dreams into Your Next Chapter,* and being a keynote speaker, I'm sharing my story here with you, too. "No knowledge is ever wasted!"

Sustaining success is a journey. Appreciate the destination points along the way. Appreciate the next chapters you get to create and find the moments of joy in the ride.

When I read the stories from Tina and Liz, I think about the stories we tell ourselves to get stuck and the stories we tell ourselves to change. As you work through Exercises 15 and 16, think about your life and your story. Have fun with these exercises. Keep in mind that life is full of infinite possibilities. If you need help, remember I'm right here with you!

POINTS TO PONDER

Think. Write. Talk. Action. *(Because practice makes us our best.)*

EXERCISE 15: This Chapter of Your Life and the Chapters That Follow

What chapter of life are you in? If your moments today were a chapter in a book, what would the chapter be titled?

_____

_____

_____

Look forward one year. What does your life look like one year from now?

_____

_____

_____

Share some success happening in your life right now that you'd like to sustain for years to come.

_____

_____

_____

What's something you don't want to change and why?

_____

_____

_____

What personal development work do you need to do to sustain success in your life?

_____

_____

_____

How long do you plan on working and what can you do to continue your professional growth?

_____

_____

_____

What good habits do you need to follow (and to be disciplined and consistent with) in your life?

_____

_____

_____

What are you willing to do differently in order to sustain success?

_____

_____

_____

What is the most difficult aspect of sustaining and maintaining success for you?

_____

_____

_____

What is one thing you would absolutely like to be remembered for in your life?

_____

_____

_____

EXERCISE 16: Journal Prompt—Your Life

Let's talk about your life as a whole, how it has gone so far and how it may go moving forward. Let's go decade by decade and write about your life, what happened in those years, and envision what will happen in the future.

0–10: (Years _____ to _____)

_____

_____

10–20 (Years _____ to _____)

_____

_____

20–30 (Years _____ to _____)

_____

_____

30–40 (Years _____ to _____)

_____

_____

40–50 (Years _____ to _____)

_____

_____

50–60 (Years _____ to _____)

_____

_____

60–70 (Years _____ to _____)

_____

_____

70–80 (Years _____ to _____)

_____

_____

80–90 (Years _____ to _____)

_____

_____

90–100 (Years _____ to _____)

_____

_____

100 and beyond:

_____

_____

CHAPTER 9
ADJUST

In the Ninth Factor of Success, we adjust. We create our own recipe for success. Here, we master our non-negotiables and method of operation with the dynamic of life changes impacting them at every point. Adjusting maintains alignment back to your vision. We learn how to adjust and reinvent. We learn how to make a change and maintain alignment to our heart, truths, and energy to make the changes.

In the 1984 Summer Olympic Games, Mitch Gaylord led the gold-medal-winning US men's gymnastics team. He was the first American gymnast to score a perfect 10.00 in the Olympics. He won the silver medal in vault, the bronze in parallel bars, and the bronze in the rings. In addition to his individual accolades, Mitch led the US men's gymnastics team to a gold medal in the team competition for the first and only time in Olympic history.

Mitch is among my favorite gymnasts of all time. I recall watching him compete on TV when I was a fourteen-year-old competitive gymnast. I sat there on the floor, in perfect splits, taking notes and knowing that I would interview him one day. Like nearly every other young female at the time, I thought I'd be married to him after watching *American Anthem*. (That gets a gigantic LOL, as I am best pals with his now wife, Valentina.)

Years later, I was working with one of my mentors, Gary Kobat, and we discussed who I dreamed of interviewing for *The Best Ever You Show*. Instantly I responded, "Mitch Gaylord!" Gary chuckled and said, "I know him personally. He is a great friend of mine." This was a dream come true, the result of serendipity, networking, and a very successful visualization.

In 2014, when Mitch appeared on my show, I had visualized the moment for years. Visualization is a powerful catalyst for adjustment and is a tool I now use daily with myself and clients. Shifting, fixing, moving, growing—everything we seek in adjustment—is made possible through seeing, or *visualizing* it . . . and that comes from tenacity.

Mitch joins us later in this chapter with his story of sustaining success over the years. He is now over sixty! I am incredibly honored to have him here with us. To sustain success over a long period of time, we must learn to navigate change.

SUCCESS TIP #65: Control the Controllables

In *The Change Guidebook*, I wrote about Ten Points of Change that I use to navigate flux. I use the book and these points in my coaching practice to help people make improvements and navigate shifting circumstances and situations.

Kate Glendon needed to make several changes in her life. Kate had hired me as her life coach and, after careful evaluation, I believed she needed a career change to leave an abusive work environment. It took considerable time for Kate to see herself clearly—the way I see her—strong, confident, funny, and capable, among many other great qualities. Today, Kate sees herself much differently than she did two years ago.

Kate describes herself prior to 2023 as a "textbook people-pleaser" who was seeking external validation due to the inability to love herself. Kate says, "It took about thirty-eight years to figure that out, but I can honestly look back and see that this journey has led me right to where I need to be to serve others as an empowerment and confidence coach. I wear my heart on my sleeve, and my kindness led me down the roads of trauma, scape-goating, mean-girl bullying, and feeling not good enough. I am a worrier; I spent many nights ruminating about any situation that did not fulfill my need for external validation."

She thinks this all started in elementary school where she wanted to be liked by her classmates. She was tall and overweight, and people bullied her. She spent years living in fear of herself and living in fear of others. Her mind was filled with doubt and concern; regardless of her accomplishments, nothing ever felt real.

Fast-forward into adulthood and working. She was obsessed with doing "the right thing" about what others thought about her, so much so that she was at war every day with herself and others. She said, "The hardest part was, as the years passed, I was worn down, developed wrinkles and gray hair, and was triggered by anything requiring me to defend myself, my work, my confidence, and my daily tasks. I was trauma-bonded to the job. The job never left my brain. I thought about it all the time, even in my dreams, so much so that for over seven years, I did not sleep past 4:00AM. I thought it was my anxiety, well it was, but it was the dirty fishbowl of an environment I was in for over eight hours a day for at least five days a week. I did not know better; I thought this was normal. I had a few not-the-nicest relationships and experiences in life but never understood that you can be content inside without it having anything to do with your professional success."

In 2021, she implemented self-love practices and learned her true value and worth. She got her power and her voice back. She discovered life coaching, which had always been an interest that she hadn't pursued. Through coaching, she had no choice but to look inward and understand how to move forward. Kate realized the unhealthy boundaries, excuses, and lies she told herself to stay in her job. Today, Kate says, "I know now I need to oversee my decisions and take responsibility for my life. I will not play the victim to my circumstances again, and I will not let another person go through life without understanding the ability to use their power. It dawned on me that I am the creator of my life."

Kate soon learned to access all the tools within that she needed to be successful.

She is so happy to have found her voice, be curious about her life again, and continue doing the look inward.

Kate also got a new therapist and finally opened up to some of her friends, who helped her understand fear versus fact, the problem with black-and-white thinking, and how to manage these experiences. Kate also took time off, something she never did before because she feared missing out at her job.

She also made changes in her lifestyle. Rather than listening to the news or music in the morning, she started each day with meditation and got ready with a podcast to calm her anxiety. Kate also stated affirmations and said three positive things before bed.

SUCCESS TIP #66: Ask Questions

In coaching, I asked very important questions for Kate to think about and answer on her own time.

Who do you want to become?

What do you want your future to be?

What do you need to do to obtain it?

Where do you want to be?

She visualized her future, felt it, and began to think of it every day.

Kate also began keeping a journal to heal and maintain alignment and mindset to be the person she was loving and discovering. Kate says, "I think kind thoughts because I am a rockstar. I love writing down everything in my head instead of fearing my thoughts. I had never journaled before; why would I want to see the words I already feel? But it is empowering to write them now and reframe them or let the thoughts run wild. I am so glad I took the time to discover myself again. Through two years of work on myself, I now have healthy boundaries, relationships, and a rejuvenating career."

Kate has also now opened her own life-coaching business and is helping others learn to love themselves and see their value and worth in all aspects of their lives.

Go Kate go! It is awesome to see Kate's coaching practice take off and see her getting that perfect mix of everything needed to help her soar to new heights.

SUCCESS TIP #67: Create Your Recipe for Success

What *is* that perfect mix to create success? So much goes into success that years back I thought it would be fun to create a recipe: a perfect blend to create success. For me, this could be my go-to for comfort, guidance, and grounding. I've added to and tweaked it over time, and it goes like this.

RECIPE TO BE YOUR BEST EVER YOU

INGREDIENTS

You
100 cups of Gratitude
50 cups of Energy
20 cups of Acceptance
20 cups of Peace
20 cups of Love
20 cups of Laughter
20 cups of Action
12 cups of Forgiveness
10 cups of Kindness
5 cups of Patience
1½ cups of Determination
1 cup of Humanity
1 cup of Confidence
1 pinch of Reality

DIRECTIONS

Ground Yourself in Gratitude.
Brew Positive Energy.
Stop Comparing.
Discover the Power of We and Us.
Find Your Best, Most Peaceful You.
Surround Yourself with Love.
Make Small Lasting Changes.
Realize Your Moments Matter.
Examine Your Positive Self.
Practice Wellness.
Be Kind.
Create a Value System for Yourself.
Create Your Best Life.

Favorite family recipes are passed from generation to generation. The recipe cards are tattered, torn, or sometimes so secret they are memorized. Excellent recipes remain with us and feed our mind, body, and spirit; they create our Best Ever You.

Elizabeth

At the end of this chapter, you'll work to create your own recipe—something to which you can refer over and over again when life throws you a curveball. When that happens, crumble it, bake it, crunch it, love it, redefine it, and honor the ooey, gooey mess that it is, and put it back out into the world with a new recipe.

Figuring out your life can be completely chaotic, let alone trying to sustain world-class success and excellence over the long term. For any and all moments, good, bad, world-class success, failure, whatever . . . I chart my course for cookies, and they are my recipe for success.

Let me explain. Chocolate chip cookies are a huge part of my life. About twenty-five years ago, I decided I would bake them not only for family and friends but would also donate them. I have baked cookies for the late, great Robin Williams through the kids' writing organization 826 Valencia. I've baked them for Little League teams, story times, weddings, schools, churches, Uncle Frank, and more. I also decided to keep a cookie count of sorts, that has added up now to tens of thousands of cookies donated across the country.

A funny thing happened along the way. People started to pay me for my cookies. I'd be retired in South Carolina right now, if I had budged and caved into all the requests for people wanting to pay me for the recipe or even pay me for cookies.

What I also learned in these moments is that I would do this whether you paid me or not. That, my friends, is called *a passion*. It honestly even took me by surprise, and I'd have to confirm it with myself and my husband more than once. Yes, chocolate chip cookies are my passion.

Here's what happens when you follow a passion. Your heart speaks, the world speaks, and things align. You will hear feedback from people—good and bad. You'll see smiles on faces, including yours. You'll learn. But most of all, you'll thank yourself and people will thank you for it.

Speaking of thank-yous, here's one of the most thoughtful hand-written notes I've ever received—and I save all of them.

Dear Ms. Hamilton-Guarino,

I am a patient at Dana-Farber and I have Stage 4 colon cancer. I have been receiving chemo for almost two years now. As you must know from leaving some cookies at the 10th floor, chemo is very hard. I also have two lovely daughters (ages eight and ten) that have been by my side and following this rough journey with me. I brought two of your cookies home to my girls who both said that they were the best cookies in the world. I want to thank you for your kindness. These little things make the road easier. My very warmest wishes to you. Thank you for your help and thoughtfulness.

This thank-you note changed my life. It made me think, not just about cookies, but how precious life and time are. I posted it on my computer, and it was there speaking to me when I started The Best Ever You Network and part of my intention and thought process in those early start-up moments.

Cookies have taught me so much about success. What *really* connects me with other people and fills my heart with joy? The answer is absolutely 1000 percent helping people be their best, and chocolate chip cookies.

Whatever it is that you do, do it with world-class excellence, success, a winning attitude, and a giant platter of cookies. I tend to think just about anything can be deemed a success when it brings happiness, joy, and smiles to yourself or others.

I wholeheartedly believe applying the concepts of gratitude-based awareness of our time, and honoring our uniqueness in the world, drive the power to create success in all areas of your life and help you sustain and carry success with you during your lifetime.

This book is here for you as a resource always also. You can turn here and look for the recipe you created to be your best or borrow mine. It will meet you in these moments and serve as a guidebook to help you become the absolute best version of yourself, and to hand-hold you through risks you may need to make to visualize, amplify, and actualize YOU, bananas, cookies, and all. Whatever it is that you LOVE, do way more of that!

My passion is helping you become your best and sustaining it.

Now, grab some cookies and milk for this next story from my friend and colleague Dr. Serena H. Huang. Serena is the former Global Head of People Analytics and HR Tech at PayPal. She also builds the people analytics functions at Kraft Heinz, GE, and Koch Industries. Serena is a regular guest lecturer at the Kellogg School of Management, the Wharton School at the University of Pennsylvania, and the Hass School of Business at the University of California, Berkeley. In 2023, I had the pleasure of training Serena Huang to become a certified professional coach. As I got to know her, I found her story more and more interesting and inspiring. I asked Serena to share her story of moving to the US at age thirteen and all that entailed.

SUCCESS TIP #68: Maintain and Sustain Your Reason Why

When Serena was thirteen, her dad announced, "We are moving to USA for a year!" He was excited about it, but Serena was not. She responded with the fight and denial you'd expect from a teenager and told her dad there was no way she was going because all of her friends were there with her in Taipei, and she loved her school.

Serena's dad worked as a professor at a top university in Taiwan his entire life. One of the incredible benefits of the academic life included sabbaticals, so he was able to take a year off from teaching and research to pursue something else. He had hired a full-service agency to look for visiting professor opportunities and help with visas, travel, and housing for the family. When he told Serena he was going to be a visiting professor at the University of Pittsburgh, she did not share an ounce of his excitement.

Four connecting flights later, as they were about to land, Serena saw cows and barns. She tugged on her dad's polo shirt and said, "Dad, I don't know anything about Pennsylvania, but I'm not sure it's known for cows." The agency had made a mistake and, instead of Pittsburgh, Pennsylvania, they landed in Pittsburg, Kansas. Pittsburg does have a university, called Pittsburg State University, which translates into the same characters in Chinese. It was too late to make changes. This was the beginning of Serena's journey in the United States.

Having grown up in the capital city of Taiwan, it was a shock to land in a town of seven thousand, with one public high school, and almost no one who looked like her. She did not speak English, which her family thought wasn't going to be problem since most schools would have English-as-a-second-language (ESOL) programs. Not in Pittsburg, Kansas, at the time. Despite there being no ESOL teacher or program to help her, Serena said, "I was determined to catch up to my classmates and took serious notes in every class. I was not shy to ask for extra help from my teachers. Plus, every night I studied the textbooks my classmates would leave in their locker."

Six months later, Serena was finally able to understand what her teachers were saying. Most importantly, she was able to communicate and started to make friends, which meant the world to a fourteen-year-old girl.

When her dad's year of sabbatical was coming to an end, she told her parents she wanted to stay in the US instead of going back to Taipei with them. They responded, "Absolutely not, you are not old enough to drive, and you can't take care of yourself."

However, Serena was determined and argued that she could continue to learn the culture and language, which would be helpful since she had planned on going to college and graduate school in the US anyway. Her parents were not convinced.

She continued, "That summer, every evening after dinner, Dad and I would take a walk to discuss this topic. He would present his arguments, and I would present my counterarguments. Finally, he said, "I cannot leave you behind. We are going home in a week." He gave me an impossible condition, "If you can find an American family that I approve of in the next seven days, after seeing their home, then I'll agree to let you stay." (Although Serena had family in Southern California, she chose not to stay with them because she said she wanted to learn English properly by being in an environment where no one spoke her native language. She said, "I was determined to make the impossible possible."

Serena learned to make adjustments, network, and navigate success at a young age.

SUCCESS TIP #69 Stay Curious

Fast-forward several years, Serena was finishing her PhD in economics at the University of Kansas shortly after the 2008 financial crisis. She applied to several jobs within a short time because she wanted to make sure she wasn't graduating into unemployment. When the university positions were canceled, she was fortunate to land a great role in consulting.

After four years in consulting, a corporate recruiter at General Electric (GE) contacted her, saying they were looking to build out "HR analytics," which she thought were not two terms that went together. She reluctantly took the call and went through the interview process simply because she was curious. She added, "I was pleasantly surprised by the leaders I met onsite in Cincinnati, who were eager and excited about what data analytics could do for human resources. I accepted the role at GE and figured I could always come back to consulting if I wanted.

"The second week I started working at GE, I had the privilege of going to the world-famous corporate university 'Crotonville.' I was so new at the company that I had no idea how special this was. Months later, I found out that our leadership team felt strongly about giving me the best new-hire experience and made a case for me to visit. It was an immersive experience of learning and absorbing the GE culture from senior leaders and corporate colleagues who had grown up at the company. Coming from consulting, everything was new, and I was intrigued by each and every conversation I had. I sent everyone I met a note to thank them for wonderful conversations, within hours of meeting them."

Over the next few years, she would be headhunted by the most admired global brands across industries, because of the personal brand she had built online. Serena became an executive at thirty-five, leading global people analytics, and started sharing knowledge on social media along with in-person conferences.

Her life was going extremely well as a data analytics executive until summer 2022, when she suddenly fell ill and eventually had to be hospitalized. Serena was forced to rest and rethink her lifestyle. In pondering what to do next, she went on a months-long self-discovery journey and realized there were two things that brought her the most joy: public speaking and creating content on social media.

"I had worked with my coach as well to figure out my values and after the health scare, my top values were health, connection, inspiration, learning, and autonomy. I went back to work for a few months and every week or so, I'd experience similar symptoms again. It was like my body was telling me the job was not aligned with my values and purpose," she said.

For the first time ever, she resigned with no job offers or even interviews lined up. She decided she would take her joy full-time and founded her own company, Data With Serena, to offer speaking and influencer marketing to the world. She had no backup plan; there was nothing to fall back on. Everyone congratulated her and said they admired her courage.

She had three clients within the first week of announcing Data With Serena. Serena admits she was not looking for validation, "But this was more than I needed to feel confident about taking the plunge into entrepreneurship. I said to myself, *If the fourteen-year-old Serena could find a family to stay with in less than seven days without Google and iPhone, there's nothing the Serena today can't do.*"

In each of the key transitions in her life, Serena said she made adjustments quickly to how she worked because she felt it was critical to get acclimated to the new environment. She added, "I credit the network around me in those moments to propel me forward faster than I could imagine, and I could not have figured it out on my own. When I transitioned from consulting to corporate, I had to learn new social norms at work to quickly build credibility. My powerful network afforded me multiple guides rather than navigating alone in the dark. When I left my corporate executive role with no backup, I reached out to the entrepreneurs in my network to get some advice. Each time I reached out, I was blown away by their willingness to help. I know I'll continue to grow and start new career chapters, and I'll have my network to support me as I go."

I'm proud of Kate and Serena who gave me permission to share part of their lives here. I trained both to be Certified Professional Coaches through Best Ever You and the Wainwright Global Institute of Professional Coaching, and I marvel at the changes they have made not only to their lives, but to those they coach.

It's time to meet Mitch Gaylord and Kelly Browne. These are two very different stories illustrating aspects of adjusting to and for success. I'm grateful they are here with us to share their stories, to show us that we aren't alone with facing and making changes.

Stories from the Heart

Mitch Gaylord—Resilience

It was the summer of 1984, the Olympic Games in Los Angeles, California, my teammates and I made history becoming the first Men's Gymnastics Team Champions and winning the gold medal. It was a surreal moment standing on the podium, singing our national anthem and watching our flag being raised in front of a sold-out Pauley Pavilion at UCLA. Millions more watched on television as I was having an out-of-body experience, a dream come true that I had worked so hard for. I couldn't believe the thoughts that were running through my head. I tried to stay in the moment and let this experience of a lifetime sink in. I couldn't help but think about the journey. It wasn't always easy, in fact there were many obstacles to overcome, challenges that I had to face, character that needed to be built. There were years of grueling training, setbacks, and disappointments that tested my inner strength. But through it all, I learned the true meaning of resilience and never giving up. That's something I'll never forget and will always be proud of, just like that moment on the podium.

Resilience refers to the capacity to adapt and recover from difficult or unfavorable circumstances. We've all experienced this in a variety of situations in our lives. In the realm of sports, it is an essential quality for athletes to possess because they frequently face physical, mental, and emotional obstacles that can impact their performance and well-being. Resilience empowers athletes to surmount challenges, rebound from setbacks, and maintain their focus and motivation when faced with adversity. By training and gaining experience, athletes can cultivate the resilience required to thrive both on and off the field. It's worth noting that resilience is a trait that people from all walks of life pursuing various goals and visions also encounter and must deal with on the road to success.

Looking back on my journey as a gymnast, one memory stands out as a true test of my resilience. It is my hope that you can take away some parts of this story that resonate with you and can put into practice the resilience you need in your life to overcome what's standing in your way. My story takes place in 1979, and I had just graduated from high school with a spring in my step and a sense of optimism for the future. I had recently won the Los Angeles City Championships and accepted a full scholarship to attend UCLA that fall. But before college began, I had my sights set on a new challenge: the USA Jr. Olympic National Championships in West Point, New York.

Competing outside of California for the first time, I was eager to see how I stacked up against the best high school gymnasts in the country. My goal was to earn a spot in the top twelve so I could participate in the two-week training camp afterwards. This camp meant everything to me, as it would provide the opportunity to work with the top coaches in the USA Gymnastics Federation and propel my skills to the next level. In addition, the top twelve athletes would be featured in *International Gymnast Magazine* as the new generation of Olympic hopefuls preparing for the 1984 Olympics.

As I trained in New York, I felt confident and ready. I had put in hours each day for months, worked on my weaknesses, and sharpened my strengths. I felt like I was as ready as I could be for this competition, however, when I arrived at the arena at West Point on the day of the competition, I felt a sudden sense of overwhelm and nervousness. The stands were packed with spectators, cameras were everywhere, and the talent of the other gymnasts I was witnessing was astounding. During the one-hour warm-up period, I struggled to maintain my focus, feeling like a small fish in a very big pond. I watched in awe as one amazing gymnast after another demonstrated skills that I couldn't believe they were able to do with such ease and accuracy. My confidence was rapidly going away, my nerves were setting in, and I could feel my palms sweating and my heart racing.

I told my coach about my doubts and fears, hoping for reassurance. He reminded me of the countless hours of practice I had put in and encouraged me to trust in my abilities. But despite his words, I couldn't shake the feeling of inadequacy that had taken hold of me. Before the competition even began, I felt like I didn't belong there. Fear of failure had taken hold of me and from that point forward I couldn't wait for this to be over.

The competition began, and I was making mistake after mistake, feeling increasingly defeated with each event. It was like I was watching the competition from the sidelines instead of being an active participant. I knew I was capable of so much more, but my self-doubt had completely taken over. When the competition was over and the results were announced, my name wasn't among the top twelve competitors. I felt devastated and like a failure, not just for myself, but for my coach and my family who had traveled all the way to New York to support me.

As I walked over to my parents for a much-needed hug, I couldn't help but feel like I had let everyone down. I didn't get to stay for the training camp I had been so excited about, and the feeling of shame and disappointment stayed with me for several days after the competition was over. As I was moping around and wallowing in self-pity, all those negative emotions somehow transformed into anger, and then into a strong and powerful feeling of determination to never, ever, have a competition like that again. I resolved to never let negative thoughts and emotions consume me to a point where I allowed them to take my inner strength and confidence to compete and perform at a level I had worked so hard to achieve. I made a vow to myself to put in maximum effort on a consistent basis, both mentally and physically, to do whatever it took from that point forward to become the best gymnast I could possibly become. At that moment, I set the goal of becoming a member of the 1984 Olympic Team just five short years away.

Obviously, I was devastated, but I didn't give up. Thought about it—but didn't give up. Instead, I used that setback as motivation to work even harder and push myself further than ever before. And you know what? That determination paid off. In the years that followed, I continued to work tirelessly on every aspect of myself, both internally and externally. You see, there's no way one's inner and outer world don't work together. In fact, it became so clear to me over the following years that my thoughts, dreams, and vision of myself and my goals were very much integrated.

Was it all smooth sailing moving forward to the 1984 Olympics? Not even close, I say with a big smile on my face. I cherished every up and down along the way knowing that as long as I stayed committed, persistent, and determined, I could weather any storm along the way, always learning from a setback and not allowing it to define me. Believe me, there were plenty more challenges, more learning experiences, some disappointing results, etc., but overall, it was a path I was committed to staying on—whatever it took to achieve the dream I set out to achieve.

In 1983, I became the number-one gymnast in the country, winning the USA National Gymnastics Championships. I was able to repeat this in 1984 as well. I had traveled the world competing in various competitions with the top gymnasts in the world and had some of the greatest life experiences as well. In the 1984 Summer Olympics, I not only realized my dream of going there, I came away with a gold, silver, and two bronze medals—much more than I ever imagined.

Standing on that podium, I couldn't help but think back to that experience in 1979 and the life lesson that it taught me—that resilience and determination can overcome even the toughest of setbacks. It most certainly was a turning point, a true test of my resilience, and it taught me that setbacks and failures are a natural part of any journey. It's how we bounce back that matters.

● ● ●

Next, please meet Kelly Browne. To me, this just wouldn't be the best book it could be without Kelly. Another author I met through HCI, I was familiar with Kelly's book series, *101 Ways to Say Thank You* and *101 Ways to Create Mindful Forgiveness,* before working with her. Kelly lives in Los Angeles and is the go-to expert on thank-you note etiquette. Now a dear friend, here she shares some incredibly difficult moments she's gone through with her family, and how she embraced her intuition, the magic of gratitude, and mindful forgiveness to successfully navigate her life.

Stories from the Heart

Kelly Browne—Dealing with and Rebounding from Devasting Events

Many years ago, I reconnected to a relative who had suffered tremendous loss. She was now calm, serene, a confident warrior, sharing that she had learned to honor, value, and embrace the shattered pieces of her life as she gathered them together into a new and perfect wholeness. With a knowing smile, she said her veins were filled with gold. It wasn't until two devastating events occurred in my life that I fully understood what she meant: my mother's death from the Aliso Canyon methane gas leak disaster, and my young daughter's catastrophic accident that broke her neck. I had to choose to adjust my entire world, ignite my intuition, and determine if I would rise up or fall to pieces—it was solely up to me. I had to be strong for the people I loved so dearly; I knew they needed me. The Japanese spirit of *kintsugi*, "to be joined with gold," teaches that no matter what painful journey one has endured, we can put the broken pieces of ourselves back together, adjusting into a more resilient, grateful, and forgiving self. I am evidence of that.

My mother would often say that "Your life can change with a phone call." There are simply no truer words. It was during one of my daily phone calls with her in fall of 2015 that I sensed something was wrong. I couldn't put my finger on it. She was dizzy, not feeling well, had headaches, and acted confused. I thought it strange that both of their dogs' ears seemed to be rotting, covered in black flies. The once lush gardens surrounding their Porter Ranch home, in Los Angeles County, had died. Blue hydrangeas, fragrant, pink-tipped queen's roses, now shriveled; the flowering jacaranda tree on the front lawn inexplicably collapsed into the street. The earth itself turned hard and lifeless. In the back of my mind, I knew something bad was happening . . . but I couldn't see what it was. My mind kept scanning for the answer, struggling to solve the problem.

I had smelled natural gas once in their backyard that faced the parched Santa Susana Mountains. I thought the heavy skunk-like odor in the air was strange, but my father reassured me that everything was secure on their property. I didn't know that hidden up in those mountains was the site of the largest natural-gas storage facility west of the Mississippi. I continued to show up on their doorstep, much to my mother's adamant concern, insisting that I go home to my precious daughters who needed me. My mind kept scanning for the answer, I couldn't turn it off. It felt like an old-fashioned radio trying to tune in to a station to get a clear reception.

Weeks before Christmas, my mother's condition worsened. She was coughing like she had bronchitis, but she didn't have a cold. Panic rose in my body as I witnessed her decline from something the doctors could not identify. By chance, I caught a news story about a gas leak in Porter Ranch. My father dismissed the possibility of a connection to my mother's health assuring, "No, SoCalGas said the leak isn't toxic and besides, it's way up in the mountains." A veteran, a family man of honor, he took them at their word. I didn't know the natural-gas blowout was coming from a well in the hills directly above them, nor that nightly well-kills were filling up the interior of their home and sickening them with dirty crude and toxins. Despite the continued safety assurances from SoCalGas, something inside me said that I had to evacuate them from the area; their lives depended on it.

While it is easy to say that nothing in the world matters more than your life, it isn't until you are faced with impending doom that you suddenly embrace the true meaning. My mother reminded me, "All of these material things we have in this life are just ours to borrow." They lost everything, and my mother was then diagnosed with end-stage cancer from the exposure. If only the doctor had believed me when I had suggested her symptoms were consistent with multiple myeloma cancer from chemical exposure! Now it was too late. I was devastated, if only I had insisted, fought harder. An invisible monster, the Aliso Canyon gas blowout lasted 111 days (from October 2015–February 2016), spewing 109,000 metric tons of methane into the environment. It was one of the worst environmental disasters in the history of the United States.

What happened over the next few years was excruciating. As we battled my mother's cancer, my gorgeous twelve-year-old daughter would be terribly injured when she was thrown from a horse at an unlicensed camp. Secretly getting to a phone and calling me for help ultimately saved her life. Despite the camp repeatedly telling me she was fine and "just homesick," something told me to go get my child. They didn't tell me she had actually suffered a violent fall. Then a parent's worst nightmare. I intuitively heard: *There's a fracture.* I didn't want to believe it, but this time I listened to that small voice in my right ear. I took her to the doctor only to discover via X-ray that her neck was broken. She was immediately strapped down to a stretcher to hold her head and neck still and an emergency trauma unit transported her through the Los Angles traffic to the hospital. There are simply no words to convey the sheer shock I went into and the powerlessness I felt, not knowing if she would survive the operation or if she would be paralyzed forever.

In those hours, I had to keep myself together, flooding the heavens with prayers for divine intervention to please save her life. We were given a miracle; she was alive and could walk. Nothing else mattered. I adjusted and remained at my daughter's side as she endured months of physical and emotional recovery.

Life brings trials and tribulations for all of us in many forms and conditions. I found that not everyone in your circle has the emotional capacity to hold your hand through the thousands of tears on a difficult journey. Friends fall away, family moves on, and marriages fail. These shattering moments were devastating, forever altering me as a human being. I am so grateful to the people in my life who adjusted their lives to hold us close to them as the storms raged and finally passed. More concerning to me was the toll of devastation and sheer fear of navigating this new life for my sweet child. While she was stitched up with a titanium implant in the back of her neck, I had to figure out how to put the broken pieces of ourselves back together again, most especially for her. With the help of a medical trauma therapy program, we immersed ourselves in learning how to recognize post-traumatic stress disorder, navigating grief for the layers of pain and suffering by adopting the calming tools of mindfulness and self-care. We learned the value of putting together what I call a "treasure box" filled with ideas, or things that give you joy—like taking a walk, enjoying a cup of tea, or mindfully eating a chocolate chip cookie. The ancients valued the power of chocolate used in religious rituals and coveted for its rich, decadent flavor, as it is calming and soothing to the soul. In my house, when we need a moment of joy, making a batch of chocolate chip cookies or sharing them with a friend in need is transformative because the love in creating and giving is contagious.

Already a devout believer in the magic of gratitude and sending thank-you notes for the simplest things in life, I treasure those blessings, being cognizant of what really matters: love and life. While I can't go back in time and save my mother or take away my daughter's pain, embracing the grace of mindful forgiveness for trauma you have experienced doesn't release the perpetrator of responsibility for the pain and suffering that they have caused, but it creates space for your personal healing. Now warrior-wise in how we see our lives and carry on with grace, we must choose joy. While difficult moments might leave you feeling shattered, take a few long, deep breaths and reconnect. When the storm is over, embrace your blessings and forgive. Always remember how beautiful the journey of life is, listen to your intuition, and know your veins are filled with gold . . . and indulge in a chocolate chip cookie.

● ● ●

I don't know about you, but one chocolate chip cookie is seldom enough! I'm honored to have Mitch and Kelly share their incredible stories. One of the best ways to remain grounded while change is brewing is with the practices of forgiveness and gratitude. They help solidify your footing in the midst of anything happening around you.

Next, let's head to Exercises 17 and 18 where you'll create your own recipe for success, and work on a journal prompt that helps you work through any adjustments or changes you'd like to make in your life.

POINTS TO PONDER

Think. Write. Talk. Action. *(Because practice makes us our best.)*

EXERCISE 17: Create Your Recipe for Success

Take a moment and create your own recipe for your best life. Use my recipe from earlier in the chapter if you need a reference. Use words from the word bank to complete the recipe. Have fun with this!

CREATE YOUR OWN RECIPE FOR SUCCESS

INGREDIENTS	DIRECTIONS
1 _____	1 _____
2 _____	2 _____
3 _____	3 _____
4 _____	4 _____
5 _____	5 _____
6 _____	6 _____
7 _____	7 _____
8 _____	8 _____
9 _____	9 _____
10 _____	10 _____

Successful Words

Ability	Authenticity	Choose	Dedication	Empower
Acceptance	Awareness	Clarity	Determination	Energy
Achieve	Awesomeness	Confidence	Devotion	Engage
Accomplish	Balance	Collaboration	Discipline	Enthusiasm
Actualize	Believe	Compassion	Discover	Excellence
Adaptability	Benevolence	Competency	Do	Faith
Align	Best	Competition	Dream	Flexibility
Ambition	Capacity	Consistency	Drive	Focus
Amplify	Change	Courage	Educate	Forgive
Assess	Character	Decide	Effort	Friendships

Successful Words (continued)

Fundamentals	Inspiring	Marketability	Purpose	Sustainability
Give	Integrity	Mentor	Read	Tenacity
Generate	Intention	Mindset	Recharge	Timing
Grace	Intuition	Miracles	Relax	Tolerance
Gratitude	Imagine	Motivation	Reliability	Trust
Ground	Impact	No	Remember	Truths
Grow	Joy	Observe	Resilience	Understanding
Habits	Judgment	Open-minded	Resourcefulness	Unique
Happiness	Kindness	Passion	Respect	Values
Harmonious	Learn	Patience	Routine	Vision
Heal	Lifestyle	Peace	Sacrifice	Visualize
Health	Listen	Percolate	Self-love	Voice
Heart	Live	Perseverance	Self-respect	Work
Honesty	Loyalty	Planning	Self-worth	Yes
Humility	Love	Possibilities	Smile	
Humor	Lovable	Potential	Spirit	
Ingenuity	Loved	Practice	Stop	
Initiative	Management	Prosperity	Support	

EXERCISE 18: Journal Prompt—Making Changes in Your Life

In your journal or below, list changes and adjustments you'd like to make, need to make, and dream of making.

Changes you would like to make:

_____

_____

_____

_____

Changes you need to make:

_____

_____

_____

_____

Changes you dream of making:

_____

_____

_____

_____

CHAPTER 10
CELEBRATE

In the Tenth Factor of Success, we celebrate. By rooting ourselves in gratitude, adjusting our perspective, and operating with a sense of abundance, peace and contentment can take hold and remain preserved in our hearts forever. Learn to celebrate wins of all sizes. Let's "TOAST" to your success!

Around thirty years ago, Wayne Connell said yes to the most extraordinary woman he'd ever known. Funny, talented, intelligent, and kind, he couldn't imagine spending another day without Sherri. They say their wedding day feels like yesterday, and Wayne and Sherri have logged many miles and overcome unimaginably high hurdles that stood in their path.

Wayne met Sherri in 1992 while she was a customer shopping at a RadioShack he was managing. At the age of twenty-seven, his bride-to-be was suddenly afflicted with a disability that changed the trajectory of her entire life, and by default, his. Diagnosed with primary progressive multiple sclerosis as well as chronic Lyme disease, Sherri's health continued to decline over the following three decades. The cruel impacts of additional ailments like traumatic brain injury, post-traumatic stress disorder (PTSD), food allergies, and multiple chemical sensitivities further deteriorated her body and psyche. Managing, maintaining, seeking comfort, and finding the finest doctors became vital for Sherri. She would later say it felt as though she'd earned a PhD in nutrition and brain science during this harrowing journey through chronic illness.

In 1996, two years after their wedding, Sherri coined the phrase "invisible disability" to describe her daily battle with debilitating symptoms that she felt and saw, yet that most others could neither recognize nor understand. Sherri used a handicapped placard to avoid long, painful walks, and yet when she and Wayne would exit their vehicle, seemingly in perfect physical condition, they were often bombarded by angry jeers and accusations of not having a disability or being in a wheelchair. These encounters and misunderstandings led the couple to take their experience public and support others who were being prejudged, disregarded, and abandoned.

Together, they founded the Invisible Disabilities Association (IDA) and began to change how the world sees disabilities, while encouraging education and connections between people and organizations touched by illness, pain, and disability. Their groundbreaking book, *But You LOOK Good: How to Encourage and Understand People Living with Illness and Pain,* has brought tens of thousands of people together worldwide to support and understand the very real consequences of quiet or unknown disabilities within our communities.

I've learned a great deal about hidden blessings from Sherri and Wayne. I've also made changes in my own life that make me more aware of my own, and how to expose them to others. Contained within the concept of hope is the vitality of sharing this joint existence with others. We often need each other to help reveal blessings, and that, too, is its own form of hope. Isolation only further burdens a disability, ailment, disease, or suffering, until hope feels buried and unattainable.

Just as Sherri and Wayne realized, perhaps your greatest gift to give and receive is to share your story of hope, how you celebrate the hidden blessings in your life, and how you found the light through darkness. Don't ever be afraid to share your hope and all the reasons why you celebrate! Better yet, be generous with the work it took to get there, for others may not yet know how to attain it for themselves.

Hope seems to innately flow from the people in these stories, like Sherri and Wayne, who take their experiences—both tragedy and triumph—and willingly share them with the world to educate, enlighten, and create opportunity. There is hope in their ability to find blessings, small and few, and magnify them until they're large enough to cover the pain, the instability of a fragile future, and the haunting fear of an unknown end result. Moment to moment, day to day, year to year, Sherri and Wayne celebrate their time together, and within that, blessings abound.

SUCCESS TIP #70: Count Your Blessings

Let their love story be a lesson in blessing counting.

Here's another pair of life change agents you should know.

SUCCESS TIP #71: Make Life Better for Those Who Need Your Help

Mark and Gail Elvidge celebrate the life-changing success they created for their son, Tanner. In 2023, they marked twenty-five years in business. Before that, Gail was a dedicated mother who didn't want Tanner to miss out on the sweeter things in life due to a life-threatening peanut allergy. She spent years researching how to safely introduce fun treats that Tanner and his friends could enjoy—and won't die from eating. It's a simple joy, and is something most people don't give a moment's thought to. Mixing, measuring, tasting, and tweaking recipes in her home kitchen, Gail sought a safe and tasty formula she could introduce to her family.

Over the next three years, Gail developed countless items that ranged from solid chocolate to molded pops and various shapes, to fruit creams, caramels, and even truffles—all crafted with great care and attention to Tanner's life-threatening food allergies. Mark and Gail started bringing their various treats to family get-togethers, parties and then, after rave reviews poured in, gave them away as gifts.

One morning as they were both getting ready for work, Mark remembers Gail talking about all the families like theirs who had the same issues with food allergies, and how difficult it was to find safe, delicious treats. "I want to start a nut-free chocolate company," she told him. He told her to do it. When Gail stepped back her comment, saying she had no idea how to start a business, Mark assured her she wouldn't be alone, that he'd help with the business end if she handled the food and creative development. That did it. In that moment, Vermont Nut Free Chocolates was born.

Gail and Mark's peanut and nut free chocolates went online in January 1998, at a time when products, particularly food, weren't moving much via computer orders—and this was the very first company of its kind. Initially, they launched the company online, direct-to-consumer only. It wasn't long before their website was discovered, and word spread among friends and support groups.

All these years later, the company has grown to a team of over thirty-five dedicated employees working hard every day to produce, package, pick and pack orders and run the administrative processes. Vermont Nut Free Chocolates takes continuous focus and meticulous preparation to deliver safe and delicious gourmet products to consumers whose health and wellness depend on the consistency of the brand. Families with food allergies—like mine—appreciate their mission and are proud to support this company, which serves customers all over the world who share this unique dietary challenge. Thank you, Vermont Nut Free Chocolates, we celebrate you!

This story illustrates another great path to success. Take an idea that fills a need or solves a problem, and act on it. Have a real-life *why* for what you do every day, and through that, find the uniqueness and intrinsic value of your product, project, or concept to carve out success. Celebrate the twists and turns along the way, just like Gail and Mark.

SUCCESS TIP #72: Celebrate *You*

Everything that happens next is because you've put in the work and committed to your success. Let yourself feel the excitement and pride of accomplishment. Be aware, grateful, and ready to embrace the possibilities of your life. It's all happening at the perfect time and you're ready to fly! Consider this book one of lessons taught and learned. Create new rules for yourself that align with what you experienced in these pages. Stick with them, be consistent. Accumulate wins and banish regrets. Think of these ideas as meaningful, mature reasons to once and for all discover everything you were born to be.

As I contemplate this for myself, I celebrate the success of shedding routine for exploration and adventure. Despite leaving the comfort and familiarity of my office and home in Maine to navigate long highways and temporary rentals, our annual trip to South Carolina has been life-changing. For six weeks, Peter and I let ourselves drift. There are no deadlines, no demands. We simply let go and allow ourselves to discover magical things about places we've never been. In that, I also learn about myself. If you think you're too old to change, or there's nothing about yourself you don't already know, I can confirm you're wrong. We are born to change, grow, evolve, and adapt, and at every stage we can be different, better, more enlightened, happier, and successful. I learned that being inquisitive and open to a new environment helped calm my mind and give me focus. I learned that sometimes being a stranger somewhere is an opportunity to hear a new story or meet a new friend. I learned that the road home doesn't have to be fraught with stress or worry. Instead, it can be peaceful to return to the place where most of your cherished memories were made.

Comfort zones aren't designed to be lived in full-time. When we seek world-class success, which by now you know means how you act, a positive mindset, strategic execution of tasks, and a gathering of supportive people, it's critical we understand and be willing to edit the usefulness of our comfort zones. When overused, they can become stagnant and confining spaces that limit our ability to connect to people and places that can change our perspectives for the better. The trick is when to sense this is happening and edit the comfort zone before it cripples us.

My southern sojourn came at just the perfect time, as my comfort zone felt like it was closing in on me, and I was pushing its foundation to expand. It may feel overwhelming or impossible to book a trip similar to mine, but growing out of your comfort zone doesn't have to look like planes, trains, and automobiles; it can be going to a movie alone, meeting a new friend for coffee, sending a résumé to a dream job, taking a class, trying a new food, or anything that is out of your norm. Use the lessons of your past to build your comfort zone, allow your vision to kick down the walls from time to time, and celebrate the unknown, for it can be a beautiful way to share yourself in ways and places that may need exactly what you can provide. That is more than a win. It's a full-circle life experience, and the absolute bedrock of strong and sustaining success.

SUCCESS TIP #73: Let Your Superpowers Shine

With success, you'll find which superpowers are unique to you. Let's figure it out. Is it your smile? Perhaps the kindness with which you interact with others. Maybe it's your ability to recognize others for their own success. Maybe you have many superpowers all combined into one special, unique you. Think of yours, and revel in them for they are usually what others either appreciate or try to diminish.

My superpower is baking chocolate chip cookies. First, to me they are a metaphor for life and breath. The other reason, and perhaps the biggest reason of all, is that cookies present a shared connection. They seldom disappoint.

SUCCESS TIP #74: Share Your Why

Chocolate chip cookies being my superpower might sound strange, but there is a reason. You see, every year, I celebrate April 10 and June 5. It's not my birthday or wedding anniversary, but rather the days I survived after nearly dying from food allergies! On April 10, 1998, I had a life-threatening allergic reaction after eating a small bag of almonds at a local coffee shop in Burnsville, Minnesota. Within a few minutes, I became dizzy, had severe stomach cramps, and noticed voices around me starting to fade and things becoming blurry. My husband carried me to the car and rushed me to the hospital, which, by sheer luck, was minutes away. We administered my EpiPen in the car and upon arrival at the hospital, my blood pressure was 65/38 and steadily dropping. I was put on a resuscitation cart. When I came back to life, I was hooked up to a variety of machines and drips and was filled with fluids that doctors had pumped into me to save my life. I spent the next several days on machines and drips designed to get my kidneys and body functioning again.

On June 5, 1999, while pregnant with Cam, our third child, I ate a chocolate chip cookie that had walnuts in it. At the time, we didn't know I had become allergic to walnuts, as these were cookies I'd eaten for most of my life. Within seconds, my unborn baby and I were fighting for our lives. The paramedics arrived and soon we were in an ambulance heading to Fairview Ridges Hospital in Burnsville, Minnesota. I was admitted and spent over a week there, hospital personnel carefully monitoring me and Cam.

These experiences changed my perspective on celebrations and how I celebrate everything in my life. Each day is one to celebrate. Each moment is one to celebrate. Knowing what it's like to nearly lose my life has made me completely understand what living is all about and how much each moment matters. I also created my sayings, "We aren't entitled to time," and "Random acts of kindness create waves of peace." In the moments that followed the last reaction, I knew I wanted to live my life differently.

SUCCESS TIP #75: Give Yourself an Internal High Five and an External Hug

I understand firsthand the challenges life can bring and have worked with people worldwide to illuminate their light within and help them uncover their best life. With me, right here, right now, find the deepest, most insecure part of yourself. Now, recognize it, accept it and make peace with it. Whatever it is or however many insecurities and challenges you have, write them down here as "I am" or "I feel" statements. If you need more room, get your journal.

For each one, give yourself an internal high five and an external hug. Believe in the power of even the tiniest accomplishment and commit to a steady diet of positivity and awareness. This practice, once it begins, will accumulate a dozen, then a series, and finally a landmark number of moments that serve as your new mindset from here forward.

SUCCESS TIP #76: Do the Gratitude Flip!

The gratitude flip shifts everything from "I have to" to "I get to." The former gymnast in me created this practice, which I maintain regularly and use to celebrate all of my blessings, gifts, flaws, and even quirks. It's a way to manage incoming fire, absorb it, and then send it back into the world as something positive and impactful. For instance, I book speaking engagements all year long, both in my home state in Maine, online for Best Ever You, or in person at another location. I speak before groups of all ages, and in all stages of life. None of them would ever report back that I appeared nervous or uncomfortable, but I have been both. It's taken me years to master the art of public speaking, which cuts many of us off at the knees. It can be pressure-packed, intensely nerve-wracking, and I vowed to get better at it to ensure my message to the audience was authentic and delivered with precision. I had to do quite a gratitude flip to get there.

If I felt insecure or anxious before a presentation, I taught myself how to take all that negative self-doubt, flip it around like the back handspring I'd learned as a kid, and exchange it for the simple gratitude of being in that place, in that moment, before that crowd. I examined the faces before me, imagining all the important pieces of their lives that I could assist with, and took many deep breaths to regulate spiking cortisol levels associated with nerves. Once I could look beyond myself, I could gratitude flip into what I needed to be for that crowd: a wise, confident contributor to their success. I once opened an event for sales professionals with an icebreaker that brought us all together in a circle to share a hug or a high five. Seeing comfort with the exercise and smiles worked like magic. I, and the crowd, knew we were all in this together.

Sometimes, taking an emotional or physical insecurity and forcing it into a gratitude flip involves making peace with an attribute or appendage you've felt disappointment with your entire life. For me, that was high heels. I'd worn them my entire life to build confidence in myself. The height they provided, the strength it took to wear them, made me walk taller and with a defined purpose. As I grew older, I got more honest: high heels hurt! Here's where I applied a gratitude flip. Instead of bemoaning the pain of high heels, I flipped that negative into a positive to appreciate the feet that carried me through years of gymnastics, motherhood, work, and long walks with my dogs. While I may not feel like I need to stuff them into heels any longer, I can reimagine all the confidence they brought me, and use that in daily life or when I'm the keynote speaker at an event or conference. The flip is what's important, not the actual act of wearing the shoes.

These little insecurities about ourselves often keep us from being our best, bold, successful selves! They can hold us back if we allow them to.

You can also turn this into a practice that is very practical in your life. If your mind wanders into negative territory or ungratefulness, bring it back by finding a positive about the situation. Flipping negatives into positives, aka the gratitude flip, takes work, but every time you force your mind to apply its purpose, you'll see it's never as bad as you thought it was at first glance.

SUCCESS TIP #77: There Are No Do-Overs

By reinforcing all factors of success, you are engaged in movement along the spectrum of full achievement. It begins with that first step and thus is vitally important to take a minute to reflect upon the feelings, failures, and repetitive actions that led you to buy this book and endeavor to create lasting, comprehensive success in your life. Take everything in, be grateful for the experiences, and celebrate two things: surviving so far, and marking a moment in your life when everything changed for the better. Be fully present and show up in each moment, with gratitude and a celebration of being *you*.

SUCCESS TIP #78: Find Your People

I want to reinforce how critical relationships, collaborations, and partnerships are in your success. Find people you relate to, and them to you. Nudge and remind yourself that not everyone will cheer you on, and emotions are as unique as fingerprints—so people often act upon them in a way that is not in accordance with your project or product. Build your closest inner circle with love, authenticity, and happiness. Cut away saboteurs who hinder your progress or inflict self-doubt. That would be anyone who imposes negativity over success or dulls your star or light.

Learn how to be selective and careful, choose who you will fight alongside in a foxhole, collaborate with on a brilliant idea, and celebrate with when dreams take shape and success is achieved.

Please meet Helen and Juli Ann Polise. They are more than just a mother/daughter duo. They are also best friends, social media content creators, and business partners.

Helen Polise is a TV commercial director turned TikTok sensation @themuthership. In 2020 when the pandemic put production work on pause, she took to TikTok to create content and have fun. She shared her life in New York City and then, using her knowledge and expertise from her thirty-plus-year career in production, began teaching her followers how to create their own videos. This new passion quickly resulted in a following of almost 1 million loyal "students" who were eager to learn how to create content from her tutorials. She was eventually approached by a venture capital team to turn her social media savvy into a startup.

Socialize was founded in 2022 with a mission of teaching creators of all skill levels how to create content for social media. Soon after launching the business, Helen partnered with her daughter, Juli Polise, who is now the chief operating officer and creative director.

Juli has worked in the social media space since graduating from the University of Michigan with her BFA in 2018. After spending a few years navigating the freelance photography and graphic design world, she worked full-time as a social media strategist, creative director, and video content creator; roles that set her up as the perfect candidate to partner with Helen in Socialize. Juli is currently residing in Los Angeles where she is also pursuing stand-up comedy and documenting the journey on TikTok.

Together, they have a podcast, *Yours Truly with Helen and Juli,* where they welcome listeners into their relationship as they tackle relatable topics with the perfect blend of laughter and tears.

Stories from the Heart

Juli Ann Polise—the Diagnosis of Success

When most people receive the news that their mom has cancer, they hardly think that diagnosis will bring success. But my mom is not like most people.

She is a force to be reckoned with, who tackles any challenge with a blinding smile, no matter the circumstances. And her cancer journey was no different.

In the spring of 2022, my mom was on a ROLL. Her successful career as a TV commercial director and producer continued to flourish as she worked with the NFL Alumni, Sensodyne, and more to create authentic advertisements. Despite being sixty-one, she had amassed a TikTok following of over half a million followers using her knowledge and expertise from TV production to teach anyone and everyone how to create content. But it wasn't just the lessons that kept followers around.

Her infectious positivity and endless energy captured followers' hearts as she also created videos about her life in NYC, dancing with her children, and just enjoying the simple moments. And if that wasn't enough, she was approached by a venture capital firm to turn her TikTok teaching into a business.

In April 2022, she was seed-funded, and Socialize Inc. was launched with the mission to be a resource for people of any age or skill level to learn how to make videos for social media. Just as she started to hit the ground running on Socialize, she began to slowly lose her vision. Day by day, her sight continued to diminish until she could hardly make out the features of a person standing right in front of her.

Despite not being able to see the screen of her phone, she continued to film and document what was happening every single day as her condition worsened. For the first time since she started TikTok, she stopped posting on a daily basis as she could not see her phone to edit and share videos.

Watching my mom go through this day by day made this the most terrifying two weeks of my entire life. She was not only my mom, but my best friend, my inspiration, my hero, and the thought of her going blind, even worse, losing her to cancer, was daunting to consider. And to make matters worse, I lived across the country in Chicago, watching and hearing all of this happen from afar.

She shared that my dad rearranged their apartment to make it accessible, and my brother came over every night just to sit with Mom and research all the medical terms and procedures on her MyChart. My brother Jonathan, who is autistic, kept her grounded with his concern about who would be taking him to the amusement park for his upcoming birthday. My role was slightly different. I was given the login information to all her e-mails and would call whenever she got an important message from work so I could help her respond.

Over two weeks and countless doctors' appointments, bloodwork, and tests later, she was diagnosed with Stage 4 non-Hodgkin's lymphoma found in the liver, and, in an extremely rare scenario, it manifested behind her eyes in her retina. Doctors were initially surprised by their findings but worked quickly to get her started with radiation on her eyes immediately to preserve any vision. But there was no guarantee.

I flew home immediately at this point to be with her for the first rounds of radiation and chemo. As soon as I landed in New York City, I felt like I could breathe again. Despite everything that was happening, my mom said I had brought a sense of normalcy back into her life. We went to brunch, I took her on long walks around the city, acting as her guide, and I even took her shopping in SoHo to find her comfy yet fashionable clothes for chemo. And one night, as we were recounting our shopping-day finds and telling my dad about the funny adventures we had, we both broke down and cried. We didn't say much, just hugged, and let ourselves release the sadness, the scary, and the unknown.

In classic Polise fashion, we decided we needed a project to focus on and together we edited all the footage she had recorded over the previous three weeks. For me, it was challenging to watch the videos, seeing the moments I had missed in person, but also the pain and struggle that was happening while I wasn't there to console. With over an hour of videos, I edited as Mom listened and we created a seven-minute-long video that documented the entire journey from day one to the day of a diagnosis.

Once it was complete, it was time to post. We decided to share it during her first chemo session, mainly because we knew we would be planted in the same room for hours, and this way we could respond to calls and messages. Especially because at the time only close family and friends knew of what was happening. No one outside of our inner circle was aware of what was going on and Helen is a pretty popular lady. How could she not be with that infectious energy!

As soon as we hit "post," the calls, the texts, the outpouring of love and support from not only friends, acquaintances, coworkers, and clients, but also from followers and strangers on the Internet poured in. It was overwhelming. The seven-minute video quickly went viral on TikTok, gaining over 350,000 views. And in that moment, my mom knew that she would continue to document her journey—the good, the bad, and the painful.

And my mom documented everything. At the beginning, I helped her create and edit videos as she was still awaiting her vision to return with radiation treatments. We went wig shopping, we spent lots of time in the hospital, but together, we weren't afraid to make jokes about her situation. This is something I get from my mother: that humor seems to be the best medicine.

Near the end of her ten-day radiation treatment, she had regained almost all of her vision. Her doctor was even surprised with how much her vision was restored. Being able to see again was the most liberating thing not only for my mom, but also our family. We were relieved that she would not be permanently impacted, but more importantly, she could continue pursuing her passion on social media.

At this point, my mom felt like she had found a new purpose in life by sharing this journey on the Internet. She was driven by a need to create these videos and share what it's like to sit and do chemo for hours, or the fear of shaving your head. A month into her cancer journey she was hospitalized for pneumonia but still continued to create and share videos from her hospital bed. Whether you are someone going through a similar health struggle, or trying to support a family member through cancer, or just want to learn how to edit videos and be entertained by a crazy lady dancing with strangers in

Times Square, my mom is driven to do that for her followers. One comment encapsulates her new purpose: "I followed you to learn about TikTok, but now I'm learning about life."

Watching my mom create videos for social media and interact with her followers is enough for me to know that she has found her true purpose in life. The pure happiness she gets from the relationships she's made through TikTok and Instagram is almost unnatural.

Now that she is cancer free, she refers to it as "the cancer thing." She celebrates being cancer free the way someone celebrates passing their driver's test. But she celebrates her followers, her passion for social media, and sharing her life like she just won the lottery, and I don't know if that would have been possible without the cancer journey.

But there was another success story that happened behind the scenes. This journey made me realize that I cannot waste a single day with my mom because it will never be enough. Since she was diagnosed with cancer, I quit my job and now work full-time with my mom at Socialize to share her video production knowledge and infectious energy with even more people.

I always knew my mom was destined for greatness, and now the whole world gets to experience it.

● ● ●

Our final contributor is comedian Amy Lyle. Amy Lyle's career highlights her talent for uncovering humor in the everyday and forging a genuine connection with her audience, whether through her written work or her live performances. She grew up in the heart of Appalachia, which is known for a population that is partial to moonshine and prone to acts of violence. Amy has penned two Amazon Humor and Entertainment bestsellers and Goodreads "Top 10 Best Humor Picks," *The Book of Failures* and *We're All A Mess, It's OK*. Amy starred in the FIIF Best Comedy Short in 2018, *The Interviewers*, and was nominated for Best Supporting Actor for the 2019 indie film *Heart of a Child*. She was invited to share her Big Idea, "Finding the Funny in the Crummy," at the 2021 Beacon Street TEDx event where she coined the phrase "Connective Humor." Amy's a reoccurring panelist for the Atlanta morning show, *Atlanta and Company*. She and her husband, Peter, are raising four children and two rescue dogs in the suburbs just north of Atlanta.

Stories from the Heart

Amy Lyle—Potholes

I want to make a movie. Specifically, a female-centric comedy that bridges the gap between working moms and stay-at-home moms. After working on the screenplay for over a year, my mentor, Rodney, e-mailed, stating, "It is done. I'll introduce you to my entertainment attorney." A few days later, I called the Santa Monica-based lawyer. He answered, "Hello, Amy Lyle, I don't care how funny your screenplay is. You're nobody, you don't know anyone, and you don't have any money, I will not represent you." In one fell swoop, I was dismissed.

Shocked, I blurted out, "That makes me really (expletive) sad!"

He laughed and replied, "I will offer you a piece of advice: write a book and get a lot of press, so 'Amy Lyle' will be associated with writing and comedy." I asked him what I was supposed to write about. He sighed, "Write what you (expletive) know," and hung up.

If a book and press could get me a movie deal, I'll write a book and get press but what would I write about? *I have had a lot of failures*, popped into my head. My life followed Murphy's general laws: "Nothing is as easy as it looks. Everything takes longer than you think. Anything that can go wrong will go wrong."

I had so many failures to choose from I didn't know where to start. I opened Google Docs and started typing. I began with growing up in Appalachia, which is known for a population that is partial to moonshine and prone to acts of violence. I moved on to marriage, surviving a divorce, being a single mom, dating while approaching forty, and getting remarried and struggling as a stepmom. I hired an editor, and she whittled my one hundred thousand words down to fifty thousand. *The Amy Binegar-Kimmes-Lyle Book of Failures: A Funny Memoir of Missteps, Inadequacies, and Faux Pas* was complete. The theme was "I am not a failure; I'm just having a little bit of trouble right now."

I sought out talented friends to brainstorm the book launch. The theme was embracing your failures and changing your life after forty. We promoted the launch with dozens of funny videos on social media, highlighting "Influential speakers, two hundred prizes, and free prosecco." We encouraged fellow high-functioning dysfunctionals to join us. Three hundred and forty-seven women (and three men) RSVP'd for the event. At the party, people lined up in front of giant book covers holding up self-selected "Failure Paddles" that read Over Spender, Exercise Hater, Grudge Holder, and Teenagers Are Tough.

There were also "Positivity Paddles" that read True Friendship, Self-Made, and My Dog Loves Me for pictures. My friend Rob deejayed and had the room dancing to Beyoncé and Madonna. It was magical. The goal was to capture the #1 Amazon bestseller badge which is awarded to the book with the highest number of sales in a specific category. The algorithm updates the best sellers' rank every hour.

At precisely 10:00 PM, my team counted down, "Three, two, one, BUY!" Hard stop—the server of the venue crashed. I was worried sick. All of the planning and expenses and not one book on Amazon had been sold. In the morning, my husband woke me up and said "Check your phone." Dozens of people from the launch party had posted pictures and videos from the launch, and dozens more were sharing their posts. By the end of the first day, almost a thousand copies had sold and *The Amy Binegar-Kimmes-Lyle Book of Failures* had earned the number-one bestselling spot in Humor Essays. My next step was to get press.

I set a goal to reach out to ten outlets a day: radio station bookers, magazine and newspaper editors, television producers, and podcasters. My booking percentage was less than 10 percent but I landed some interviews and features including the *Atlanta Journal-Constitution*, NPR, LA Talk Radio, many local magazines, and eventually, the book title landed a mention in *The New York Times*. "Failing Forward" was a trending topic, and I was able to book guest spots on Atlanta morning shows. After a three-minute interview on *Atlanta and Company*, the producer asked if I could stay for their end-of-the-show segment, *Real Talk*. It featured the two hosts plus two guests discussing current issues. Unexpectedly, a few weeks later, the producers invited me to join *Real Talk* again. Being a panelist resulted in a twice-a-month invitation for three years. The *Real Talk* panelists, primarily women, evolved into a kind of sisterhood. Among them were leaders of substantial women's groups, contributors to various magazines and blogs, hosts of their own TV shows, and creators of podcasts. This group fostered a sense of camaraderie, where we supported each other's endeavors and projects.

Meanwhile, a brilliant woman who previously had worked for a Steven Spielberg company and had started working on independent films, had moved into my neighborhood in Georgia. We were introduced by a mutual friend. She agreed to produce my female-centric comedy that bridges the gap between working moms and stay-at-home moms, and secured Hollywood money. We were discussing Georgia film tax incentives when she checked her phone to see notifications about Georgia's plan to restrict reproductive rights. She expressed her concern saying, "I hope this bill will not impact our funding."

I said, "I'm sure it won't." It did. The next day, Alyssa Milano kicked off a "Boycott Georgia Film" campaign on X (previously Twitter). Our funding, as well as the funding of many independent projects, was pulled. The producer moved on to another project and shortly after relocated to another state. I was back to ground zero.

I didn't want to give up on my film dream, but it was on hold for now. I was promoting *The Amy Binegar-Kimmes-Lyle Book of Failures* on social media by posting a weekly "Friday Fail." Often, my funny failures inspired people to share their own faux pas. Their failures were so hilarious that I reached out to them for details. If a story had legs, I'd ask the creator's permission to edit their story, use their name, and put it in a book. Ninety percent said, "Sure!" The second book, *We're All a Mess, It's OK*, practically wrote itself.

I was on the hunt for an eye-catching book cover and enlisted nine close friends and one alpaca. A friend tagged me on a viral video about therapy llamas at a children's hospital. She jokingly suggested, "Why not get a llama for your book cover shoot? It would be hilarious." Surprisingly to me, North Georgia boasted fifteen llama and alpaca farms, but they advised against studio settings for these camelids due to safety concerns. I was about to break the news that I could not secure a llama when an animal casting agency finally responded, offering a llama for an hour for five thousand dollars. We eventually settled on an alpaca for fifteen minutes for five hundred. The day of the shoot arrived, and a handler emerged from a trailer, leading an adorable lady alpaca with a super fluffy mane, impossibly long lashes, and an endearing underbite. The excitement among us was palpable. The alpaca, however, grew uneasy on set, darting about and delivering potent kicks—our plan to center her amidst us quickly unraveled. In a spontaneous adjustment, four of us sat on a sofa while the trainer crouched behind, managing the alpaca's reins, and miraculously, we captured the shot we needed.

Becky, the friend who proposed the alpaca for the cover, also sparked the idea of a marketing campaign for *We're All a Mess, It's OK* featuring a talking alpaca as a mascot. Taking a static image of the alpaca, we used software to give it a voice. Chris Corso, a talented voice-over actor, brought "Santiago" to life. He recorded witty excerpts from the book in a delightful Peruvian accent, always concluding with a heartfelt "I love you; I love you so much." The strategy paid off. *We're All a Mess, It's OK* soared to number one across multiple categories on Amazon and snagged a spot on Goodreads' Top 10 Best Humor list. The adoration for "Santiago" prompted a flood of alpaca-themed gifts—notebooks, earrings, socks, even Christmas cards and underwear—from fans. It's incredible how a spontaneous, last-minute idea evolved into something wonderful.

Unexpectedly, Sam, an Atlanta filmmaker who had seen me on a local TV show, asked if I would consider starring in a film short playing a recruiter. I'd never been in a film, but for almost a decade, I had been volunteering for a huge non-profit as the opening act for their children's ministry and, professionally, I'd been in the recruiting business for over fifteen years, so I said yes.

During the downtime on *The Interviews* set, I met a film director, who asked if I would be interested in playing a therapist for the 168 Film Project. Although I was compensated in tacos, it led to roles in several independent films including a SWAT member, mad scientist, assistant to an evil ruler, and a commercial for a T-shirt company. A year later, Sam's film short won Best Comedy at the Franklin International Independent Film Festival, and he achieved his goal of attracting representation. While on set, a producer asked him if he knew of any comedy scripts; he took the opportunity to pitch my project. Remarkably, I once again had representation for the full-feature, female-centric comedy that bridges the gap between working moms and stay-at-home moms.

My new producer, who had sold over forty film projects, wanted to break into television and asked if I would change the full feature to a sitcom and invited another writer to the project. It took about a year to rewrite the feature into pilot form, prepare the marketing deck, and research a list of potential buyers before she could begin to pitch. So far, this has been my Hollywood experience: a production company/network engages with my producer with e-mails that say things like, "We love it." "We can see getting at least eight seasons out of it." "We will attach a well-known female director," and, "We have a star in mind that would be perfect for this project." However, after those promising exchanges ... silence.

I welcomed the distraction from my lack of sitcom success when a financial planner asked me to speak at an event. Then, a large real estate group and a few women's groups invited me to speak. I enjoyed speaking and I was making a little bit of money. I thought that perhaps I could take it to the next level, but I would need to break into the highly competitive speakers' circuit. I set a goal of landing the Super Bowl of all speaking engagements: a TED Talk. I applied to over eighty venues before getting invited to

Beacon Street's April 2020 TEDx event. I dreamed that my Big Idea of "Finding the Funny in the Crummy" would start a movement, with millions of people changing their lives by embracing the healing power of "Connective Humor." I would be offered thousands of dollars as a keynote speaker and be able to attract a buyer for my female-centric comedy.

But . . . COVID.

Due to the pandemic, the live event was canceled. Consequently, speakers were required to record their own talks. While the talks were scheduled to go live in early 2020, I wasn't able to find my presentation on the event's website. It later emerged that the organizing group, facing a shortage of staff, hadn't updated their speakers' talks for two years. As a result, the talks were simply uploaded to the general TEDx YouTube page, among the other hundred thousand talks. Although participating in a TEDx in any capacity is an incredible opportunity, at that moment, I was crushed. Doors kept opening, but they were only cracked, and then closed.

Before the pandemic, I was doing a lot of stand-up comedy in Atlanta. I was also writing and co-hosting a Roku show for a local network and wrote a monthly segment for a magazine. All were now canceled or on hold.

I admit that I was in a "woe is me" state of mind when I invited my most encouraging friend to lunch. I started listing where I had fallen short. I'd sold a lot of books, but the marketing costs ate up the profits. I was still being compensated for acting roles with snacks. The Roku show was canceled, and the magazine opportunities had slowed. I hadn't broken into the speakers' circuit, and, finally, I hadn't sold the female-centric comedy that bridges the gap between working moms and stay-at-home moms. I was also perimenopausal and sweating heavily. Woe is me, woe is me.

My friend took a deep breath and exhaled. She took my hands in hers and said, "God put you on this earth to make people feel better about their lives; that's your gift, and with every book, talk, appearance, article, and stand-up set, you're using your gift. Dear friend, is not the journey the reward? Why are you only focused on the potholes?"

My friend had disrupted my definition of success. It finally hit me. Like many, I found myself plagued with the "if only" syndrome. I believed that success and happiness were contingent upon the production of my film, securing a larger project, a material object, or shedding ten pounds. I kept moving the finish line, trying to prove that I was good enough from both real and imagined critics. I've experienced opportunities that most people only dream about. I've developed friendships with talented, courageous, and generous creatives. My work was making people feel better about themselves. My husband likes me, my rescue dogs love me, and my children are unafraid to pursue their dreams because they've grown up watching me pursue mine. There is much to celebrate. It is a journey, and every step deserves celebration: conquering challenges, moving forward, and, above all, the inspiration you've found and shared along the way.

My hope for you, as you have read the incredible stories in this book, is that you had many "it hit me" aka "aha" moments. And as you Imagine, Believe, Focus, Plan, Ask, Network, Collaborate, Sustain, and Adjust, that you do not skip the last element: to Celebrate. Take the time to pause and celebrate even the smallest wins, embrace your imperfections, enjoy chocolate chip cookies, and appreciate the journey. Underdogs unite!

● ● ●

Underdogs unite is right! Thank you for sharing your stories, Juli, Helen, and Amy.

As we wind up here, I wanted to share a few final success tips with you.

SUCCESS TIP #79: Celebrate the Dreams That Come True

As I was finishing up the book, I caught this LinkedIn post from Jesse Cole of The Savannah Bananas. It's a solid reminder that your craziest ideas, wildest dreams, or however that gets phrased in your mind, do come true—and they still aren't about dollars in your pocket but rather smiles on faces.

> Are you kidding me!? You couldn't write it up much better than this . . . a young fan caught a foul ball to end the game last night. In Banana Ball, if a fan catches a foul ball, it's an out . . . but to get the final out by catching a foul ball and securing the win for the Bananas was absolutely wild. When we first came up with this rule, I pictured this exact moment. I envisioned a fan catching the ball to win the game and the players bringing the fan on the field to celebrate and the whole stadium going crazy! That's exactly what happened. This Banana Ball Tour has brought so many epic moments, but this was a moment I'll never forget. This young fan was treated like a hero by not only the players but all the fans who gave him high fives and congratulated him as he left the ballpark.

He was treated like a legend and deservedly so after the amazing play to win the game.

SUCCESS TIP #80: Celebrate Others

Like Jesse says, "Fans first." This motto is not about Jesse. Remember in all these celebrations, that so much of life isn't about you. In fact, another's win might be your very best day. If you aren't having the success you hoped for in this moment and someone else is, celebrate them. Your time will come. In those moments, remember, when you feel passed over, uncelebrated, jealous, understated, overlooked, under-appreciated, ungrateful, unloved, or any other of the words that undo gratitude and your best success, to understand that you are enough and to not be jealous of others' success. Don't get stuck in woe-is-me mode. Remember to look within for the answers. Remember that when you look externally and compare yourself to the success of someone else, you block gratitude.

Remember to help others be bold and brave. Help them do what you can do and know what you know. Your smile is a game changer. Your time is life-altering, and you always have the superpower within to help another person in ways that take just a bit of your time and energy. Look in the everyday and ordinary for the extraordinary.

As you do this, you'll connect with your true self and to others around you and in turn to the world as a whole in peace for peace. Embrace your inner love, gifts, and talents that are the essence of who you are and share your uniqueness with the world.

Visualize your success.

Actualize your success.

Amplify your success.

The world needs a more authentically aligned you.

By the way, we arrived home in Maine today. We took more than a week to return home with stops in Washington, DC, to see Cam and the Hoyas, as well as family in New Jersey. We are grateful and happy to be home. We are greeted first by Quinn's dog, Harley, who has learned to howl, and it is adorable. Next, Quinn smiles and we give him giant hugs and thanks for holding the fort down. The cats are coming one by one to say hello and we are once again surrounded by the comforts of home, even with the "snowicane" headed our way. I've traded in my swimsuit and sandals for a shovel and snow boots and found success in knowing all we've accomplished and the collaboration and love that went with it. Endings are always reflections, blessings, and new beginnings.

Love to you all and thank you so much for being here with me. I will be celebrating YOU!

I'd like to leave you with this:

Here's a **TOAST** to expanding your success and capacity for growth! You did it! You recognize that consistent personal growth coupled with ongoing successful results require leveling up in these powerful, yet key, inner-character traits:

TRUST. Having faith in yourself by behaving beyond your level of trauma. Reducing and/or removing fear and wounds as an excuse not to trust.

OPEN-MINDEDNESS. Being open to learn. Learning new perspectives opens up pathways to infinite opportunities, more successes, and peace.

ALIGNMENT. Connecting to our real selves versus our egoic selves so that we may authentically follow our heart, truths, and higher energy versus living story after story, through excuse after excuse.

SELF-WORTH. You're enough. Always have been, always will be. Lead with an awareness of and connection to your value, intelligence, creativity, and ability to learn, in a worthy and deserving way.

TRUTH. Embracing and facing your authenticity when things have happened in your life FOR you, not TO you. Be generous in sharing those lessons.

POINTS TO PONDER

Think. Write. Talk. Action. *(Because practice makes us our best.)*

EXERCISE 19: Yay You!

1. What accomplishments have you achieved, and how are you celebrating those successful milestones?

_____

_____

_____

_____

_____

2. What brings you joy?

_____

_____

_____

_____

_____

3. Describe a small or big win that you've had recently. What's going well in your life?

_____

_____

_____

_____

_____

4. If you were to take one step today to take all you've learned and create a positive impact on others, what would you do?

_____

_____

_____

_____

5. What is an area of your life in which you feel you've made progress but there is still work to be done? Describe the area and the improvements you are making.

_____

_____

_____

_____

EXERCISE 20: Journal Prompt—The Extraordinary in the Ordinary

Take your everyday, ordinary life and write about all the things that are extraordinary. Count your blessings.

_____

_____

_____

_____

_____

_____

_____

_____

_____

_____

_____

BEST EVER YOU TOOLBOX

Summary Part 1: Visualize Your Success

In Chapters 1–3, you imagine, believe, and focus to form the practice of imagining what you want to achieve. This involves using the strength and confidence within you to create desired outcomes, goals, or positive changes in your life. You acknowledge and live your superpowers to maintain and sustain your dreams and goals in the face of naysayers, adversity, or other obstacles. You have confidence, uniqueness, growth, awareness, and a keen understanding of values, goals, beliefs, and behaviors. You know the process, effort, and commitment it takes to bring success into your life. You define what success looks and feels like to you personally.

Elizabeth's Bookshelf

Sophia A. Nelson: *The Woman Code: 20 Powerful Keys to Unlock Your Life,* and *Be the One You Need: 21 Lessons I Learned While Taking Care of Everyone but Me*

Jesse Cole: *Fans First: Change the Game, Break the Rules & Create an Unforgettable Experience*

John Wooden: *Coach Wooden's Pyramid of Success*

Joe Sperle: *Athlete's Guide to Success: A Roadmap to Becoming a Champion*

Emily A. Francis: *The Taste of Joy: Mediterranean Wisdom for a Life Worth Savoring*

Cal Newport: *Deep Work: Rules for Focused Success in a Distracted World*

Summary Part 2: Actualize Your Success

In Chapters 4–6, you plan, ask, and network to heighten your awareness and create steps toward tangible achievements. Here you develop and realize your full potential and become the best version of yourself. Success isn't a solo effort and here we learn to establish a plan, ask beyond our circle of who we know, and network for our best route to success. We step out of our comfort zone when needed to build strong relationships with others based on respect and trust.

Elizabeth's Bookshelf

Jack Canfield: *The Success Principles: How to Get from Where You Are to Where You Want to Be*

Miriam Laundry and Jack Canfield: *I Can Believe in Myself*

Merril Hoge: *Find a Way: Three Words That Changed My Life*

Del Duduit: *Dugout Devotions: Inspirational Hits from MLB's Best*

Ivan Misner: *Who's in Your Room? Networking Like a Pro*

Congressman Ric Keller: *Chase the Bears: Little Things to Achieve Big Dreams*

Lisa Gable: *Turnaround: How to Change Course When Things Are Going South*

Kelly Browne: *101 Ways to Create Mindful Forgiveness: A Heart-Healing Guide to Forgiveness, Apologies, and Mindful Tools for Peace*

Jesse Cole: *Find Your Yellow Tux: How to Be Successful by Standing Out*

Summary Part 3: Amplify Your Success

In Chapters 7–10, you collaborate, sustain, adjust, and celebrate to enhance certain aspects of your thoughts, feelings, or behaviors to create positive change, longevity, and continued personal and professional growth. Amplifying your success involves maintaining your vision and focusing on the strengths, resources, and opportunities to foster success at all points in your life. As you do this, you remain flexible to alter your course, goals, and strategies when needed. Here, we celebrate achievements and accomplishments of all sizes.

Elizabeth's Bookshelf

Wayne Connell: *But You LOOK Good: How to Encourage and Understand People Living with Illness and Pain*

Sally Huss: *A Most Extraordinary Life: A Champion's Journey from Wimbledon to Hollywood, from Aspen to Amazon*

Tina Sloan: *Changing Shoes: Staying in the Game with Style, Humor, and Grace*

Liz Brunner: *Dare to Own You: Taking Your Authenticity and Dreams into Your Next Chapter*

Jesse Cole: *Banana Ball: The Unbelievably True Story of The Savannah Bananas*

Amy Lyle: *We're All a Mess, It's OK: A Collection of Funny Essays and One-Liners About the Struggles of Everyday Life* and *The Book of Failures.*

Chris Crowley and Dr. Henry S. Lodge: *Younger Next Year for Men* and *Younger Next Year for Women*

DISCUSSION AND OPTIONAL MASTER CLASS CERTIFICATION

· · · · · ·

For those who wish to obtain a Best Ever You Success Master Class Certification, please submit your answers to the questions below at this website: BestEverYou.com/SuccessGuidebook.

For those wishing to just continue and enjoy learning about success or use this for a book club or work-related discussion, these discussion questions are here for you to complete at your own pace.

1. What is a valuable lesson or two that you learned from Part 1: Visualize Your Success.
2. What are the Ten Factors of Success?
3. What is the purpose of the Ten Factors of Success?
4. Which factor resonates with you the most?
5. What is your definition of success? What does success mean to you personally and professionally?
6. What is a valuable lesson or two that you learned from Part 2: Actualize Your Success?
7. Who has helped you in your life? How have they helped?
8. What has gone according to plan in your life and what has not?
9. Is there anyone you wish you could network with and know?

10. What is a valuable lesson you learned from Part 3: Amplify Your Success?

11. Do you need to change anything about yourself or any situations in your life?

12. Describe a successful collaboration in your life.

13. Do you fear any aspects of collaboration? Why?

14. What do you need help with this next year?

15. What are a few of your biggest achievements or triumphs this year?

16. What have you learned about yourself by reading this book?

17. What is your superpower and how are you using it to benefit others?

18. What is your ideal day and your favorite way to celebrate you?

19. Which two stories from the book did you enjoy the most and why?

20. Where do you want to be next year?

Bonus Question:

1. Would you share this book with someone else and tell them about it? What would you say?

ABOUT THE AUTHOR

In 2008, Elizabeth Hamilton-Guarino closed the door to her office to think about her life.

When she opened it, she walked through, leaving behind an almost two-decade career in the financial services industry in order to open the doors for The Best Ever You Network. Today, Best Ever You is a multimedia brand and platform with millions of fans and followers around the world.

Elizabeth is a tireless champion of others and believes in the need for the individual light within to raise the collaborative power of us and we.

Today, Elizabeth is a writer, master coach, and speaker focused on change, success, gratitude, and helping people be their best. She is the author of the bestselling and five-time award-winning book, *The Change Guidebook: How to Align Your Heart, Truths, and Energy to Find Success in All Areas of Your Life.*

Elizabeth is also a frequent speaker, and her work has been featured in places like *Good Housekeeping, US News and World Report, Forbes, Thrive, Medium*, and more. Her popular "4-4-4 Newsletter" is sent out each week to thousands of subscribers.

Elizabeth and her husband, Peter, have been married for more than twenty-five years and have four adult sons, three rescued cats, and two dogs. They can often be found in their gardens, in the pool, raking leaves, or, depending on the season, in Myrtle Beach, South Carolina.

You can learn more and sign up for the e-newsletter at elizabethguarino.com and by visiting BestEverYou.com.